THIS BLESSED LAND

CRIMEA AND THE CRIMEAN TATARS

THIS BLESSED LAND

Crimea and the Crimean Tatars

Paul Robert Magocsi

Distributed by the University of Toronto Press

for the

Chair of Ukrainian Studies

University of Toronto

2022

Publication of this volume was made possible
by the generous support of the
Ucrainica Research Institute
Toronto, Canada

Library and Archives Canada Cataloguing in Publication

Magocsi, Paul R., author
This blessed land: Crimea and the Crimean Tatars
/ Paul Robert Magocsi.

Includes bibliographical references.
ISBN 978-0-7727-5110-2 (bound)

1. Crimea (Ukraine)—History. 2. Tatars—Ukraine—
Crimea—History. I. Title.

DK508.9.K78M33 2014   947.7'1   C2014-900066-9

Maps by Paul Robert Magocsi
Design and layout by Larysa Ilchenko

First edition published 2014
Reprinted with corrections 2022
© Governing Council of the University of Toronto

Printed in the Czech Republic
ISBN 978-0-7727-5110-2

CONTENTS

LIST OF MAPS

What is Crimea?

A land drenched in warm sun. A land swept by tropical breezes laced with fragrances from a wide variety of grasses, trees, plants, and the spices they produce. A land whose extensive shores are washed by mildly salted seas that invigorate both body and soul. This is Crimea.

A virtual island set off from the rest of the European continent, Crimea exudes an all-persuasive sense of tranquility. In the words of one perceptive observer, Crimea's "beauty provokes almost sexual yearnings of possession" in all who have been entrapped by its lure.[1]

For all these reasons Crimea has for over three thousand years continued to attract numerous peoples to its steppelands, mountains, and seashores. And it is the story of these peoples and the civilizations they created that is the subject of this book. Hopefully, the pages that follow will provide through text and images a suitable introduction to readers who have never been to Crimea as well as to those who have been already and who surely will want to return.

View of Mt. Aiudag from the nearby coastal town of Hurzuf.

Chapter 1

Crimea: the Land and its Seas

Crimea is an autonomous, or self-governing republic within the independent state of Ukraine. In terms of physical geography, Crimea is a peninsula in the shape of an irregular quadrangle that is surrounded on virtually all sides by water: to the west and south by the Black Sea; to the east by the Kerch Straits; and to the north by the Sea of Azov, as well as the Sivash or Putrid Sea which is, in fact, a shallow body of unnavigable water comprised mainly of lagoons and marshes. At one point along its northern edge Crimea is connected to the Ukrainian mainland by a narrow strip of land called an isthmus near the small settlement of Perekop. For centuries the only connection between Crimea and the rest of the European continent was, indeed, through the Perekop isthmus. A bit east of Perekop there are two narrow straits near the mainland villages of Sivash and Chongar. Only in modern times were these shallow waters crossed by railroad and automobile bridges, which since then have provided an alternate connection for Crimea to the Ukrainian mainland.

Crimea measures only 25,900 sq. kilometers (10,100 sq. miles), which makes it about the size of Maryland in the United States, or the country of Macedonia in Europe. With regard to its geography, it is comprised of three distinct zones: a steppe-like lowland plain, mountains, and a coastal shoreline. By far the largest of these zones is the Crimean lowland, which covers the northern two-thirds of the peninsula. This is a flat, treeless plain subject to frequent and often violent winds. The farthest eastern extension of the lowland plain is known as the Kerch Peninsula, which culminates at the Straits of Kerch, a narrow body of water which connects the Sea of Azov to the Black Sea and also forms the international boundary between Ukraine and Russia.

The other two geographic zones comprise the southern third of Crimea. These include the foothills and three parallel ranges running west to east of the Crimean Mountains. The highest of the three is the southernmost, or coastal range, known as the Yaila (the Tatar word for alpine pasture), noted for its

◀ *The Khroni promontory along the northern edge of the Kerch Strait as it flows into the Sea of Azov.*

MAP 1

CRIMEA: PHYSICAL GEOGRAPHY

SEA OF AZOV

Kerch

Kerch Straits

KERCH PENINSULA

Feodosiya

Canal

Staryi Krym

Sudak

SEA

Crimean

Bilohirsk

CRIMEAN MOUNTAINS

Chatyr-Dag 1527

Roman-Kosh × 1545

Simferopol

Yalta

Chongar

Sivash

Dzhankoi

Krasnohvardiiske

Bakhchysaray

Alma

Ai-Petri × 1234

LOWLAND

North

Inkerman

Perekop

Armiansk

Krasnoperekopsk

Sevastopol

Balaklava

Canal

Black Sea

Yevpatoriya

BLACK

Dnieper

Elevation (m)

1200 m
900
600
300
Sea level

Boundary between Ukraine and Russia

Boundary of the Autonomous Republic of Crimea

Canals

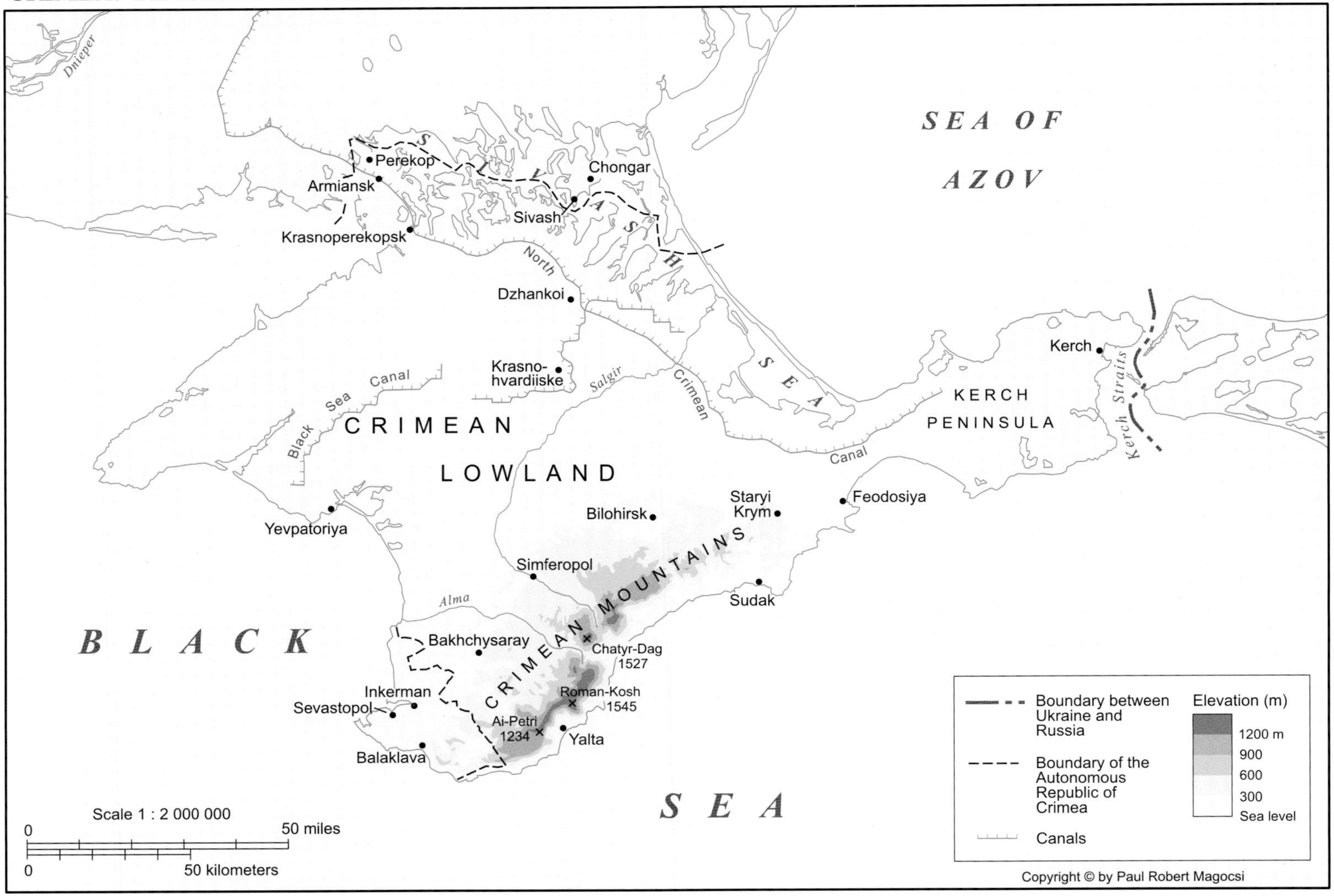

Copyright © by Paul Robert Magocsi

SEA

Scale 1 : 2 000 000

50 miles

50 kilometers

View of the Ashama-Dere ravine from the cave-town Kirk Yer/Chufut-Kale.

several table-like massifs ranging from 1,200 to 1,400 meters above sea level and punctuated by a few rugged peaks, the highest of which are Roman-Kosh (1,545 meters) and Chatyr-Dag (1,527 meters). The Yaila range forms a kind of backdrop, or a wall of cliffs facing the Black Sea, which provide a protective shield for Crimea's third geographic zone, the littoral or coastal region. This zone consists of a narrow strip of land, ranging no more than 2 to 12 kilometers in width, which stretches for about 150 kilometers along Crimea's southern coast. It is along the coastal littoral that Yalta and other famous resort towns are located, as well as several port cities like Sevastopol, Sudak, Feodosiya, and, at the eastern end of the peninsula, Kerch. All these ports, although under different names, have functioned as im-

portant political, economic, and cultural centers from pre-historic times to the present. In many ways, this third geographic zone of Crimea is a far eastern European version of the better known French and Italian Rivieras, which, like the Crimean Riviera, also form a narrow coastal littoral along the Mediterranean Sea separated by the Alps from the northern hinterland regions of Provence and Piemonte/Piedmont.

Also like the Mediterranean Riviera, Crimea's littoral is blessed with a mild climate, with temperatures that are never below freezing in winter (on average 4 °C in January) and that approach subtropical conditions during the long rainless summers whose considerably higher temperatures (on average 24 °C in July) are moderated and made comfortably tolerant by steady breezes from the

Black Sea. By contrast, the mountainous geographic zone receives higher levels of precipitation and is much colder in winter (on average −4 °C in January) when snowfalls are quite common. Finally, the lowland steppe is usually quite hot and dry, especially during the summer months (on average 22 to 24 °C in July), when it receives a limited amount of rainfall and is lacking in the moderating sea breezes.

The geographic and climatic conditions in the Crimea have, not surprisingly, influenced human settlement patterns. The mild Mediterranean climate, especially along the coastal littoral, has for thousands of years attracted in-migration from colder continental climates farther north. The coastal zone has also witnessed a regular cycle of growth, decline, and re-birth of coastal port cities settled by merchants and artisans whose economic livelihood has been dependent on the Black Sea and on lands farther south along the coasts of the Aegean and Mediterranean seas. In that sense Crimea has for most of its history functioned as a transitional socioeconomic zone connecting the Eurasian steppe hinterland with the Mediterranean-Aegean civilizations of ancient, medieval, and early modern Europe.

The warm southern slopes of the Crimean Mountains that protect the coastal region have also for centuries attracted farmers, who have cultivated a wide variety of fruits, vegetables, tobacco, and most especially grapes to produce wines for which Crimea has become world famous. By contrast, the

Sub-tropical vegetation at the Livadiya Park.

6

View in the distance of the Kara-Dag mountain range in southeastern Crimea.

mountains, in particular the tabletop formations of the Yaila ranges, have provided refuge for peoples seeking protection and, therefore, have in the past served as the location for numerous fortress settlements and centers of relatively isolated political entities. Finally, Crimea's northern lowland steppe zone has traditionally been attractive to nomadic peoples and tribal-groups whose livelihood was traditionally connected with animal husbandry.

Even more diverse has been Crimea's human geography. The list of peoples who have made the peninsula their home is mind-boggling. Representatives from virtually every linguistic and cultural group in Europe and Asia have left their mark: beginning with the Taurians, Scythians, Greeks, Sarmatian Alans, and Romans of antiquity, and continuing in medieval times with Byzantine Greeks, Goths, Khazars, Kipchaks, Mongols, Tatars, Seljuk and Ottoman Turks, Genoese, Venetians, Armenians, Crimean Jews, Greeks, Bulgarians, and Germans, and in more modern times with Russians, Ukrainians, and the political "tribes" of the twentieth century: "White" and "Red" Russians as well as various "Soviet" peoples. It is to the historical evolution of these various peoples and the civilizations they created in Crimea that we now turn.

The birth of the land of beauty

Crimea's maritime landscapes seem to be the very embodiment of eternal beauty—the mountainous rocks covered with dark green vegetation are as ancient as the blue sky and the sun that shines over them. It is difficult to believe that in geological terms the Crimean peninsula is relatively young, having been formed only about 8,000 years ago. Before then, Crimea was little more than the elevated part of the northern bank of the Black Sea, which at the time was a huge fresh-water lake.

When the glacier that covered most of continental Europe retreated, the waters of the Mediterranean and Aegean Seas broke open a channel that eventually formed the Dardanelles, the Sea of Marmora, and the Bosporus, through which salty water flowed northward into the fresh-water lake which became the Black Sea. Some authors have associated this major catastrophe with the stories of Noah's Flood in the Bible and the Dardanus Flood in the mythology of the ancient Greeks.

Today most scholars take a more moderate view, which suggests that the water level of the Black Sea rose only gradually and over several decades, if not centuries. Nevertheless,

The Sea. Crimea, *painting (1898-1908) by Arkhyp Kuindzhi.*

it seems that precisely these events shaped Crimea as a peninsula and virtually separated it from the mainland to the north. During this process the salty water and fresh water did not mix, but rather created two separate layers in the sea: the upper, salty layer about 90 meters (280 feet) deep, and the lower, fresh-water layer just beneath it. When the once abundant vegetation at what became the bottom began to rot, the fresh water was gradually saturated with poisonous gas, including hydrogen sulphide, which makes impossible for any form of organic life to exist. In short, while in the upper, salt-water level there was always an abundance of fish and maritime life, beneath the ninety-meter level there was only "dead" water.

Hydrogen sulphide is, however, an excellent preservative, so that archeological objects which would otherwise disintegrate in salty sea water were "saved," transforming the Black Sea into a paradise for latter-day underwater archeologists. For political and financial reasons, the seascape around Crimea has only recently begun to be studied in a systematic manner. The importance of such research for Crimean and general Ukrainian history is difficult to overestimate, since the earliest human settlements in this region were most likely located on the bottom of what is now the Black Sea.

Every sea is a dynamic system, and sometimes during severe storms hydrogen sulphide reaches the surface of the water. This is visible from the shores of Crimea as a kind of purple sheen on the surface of the water. Since poisonous gas burns when exposed to open air, the purple spots on the sea surface can at times burst into flame. It is especially under dark stormy skies that these sea-fires impress the modern-day observer. One can only imagine the shock such fires provoked in the souls of sailors from the ancient past. Then, as now, the Black Sea continues to offer up mysteries that excite the human imagination.

Nadiya Kushko

Chapter 2

Crimea's earliest civilizations

Since pre-historic times, Crimea has functioned as a transitional zone connecting the steppe hinterland of southern Ukraine with the Black Sea and beyond. Maritime communication farther southward across the Black Sea and through the straits of the Bosporus and Dardanelles that separate Europe from Asia has provided Crimea with access to the lands and civilizations that have flourished since antiquity along the shores of the Aegean and Mediterranean Seas.

For nearly three millennia, from about 1150 BCE (before the Common Era) to the 1700s CE (the Common Era)—a period in European civilization divided chronologically by the birth of Christ and therefore also identified as BC (before Christ) and AD (*anno domini*, in the year of Our Lord)—Ukraine's steppe hinterland was home to a series of nomadic tribal groups, most of whom originated farther east in Central Asia. Among the earliest of these historically known groups from the east were the Cimmerians, who arrived in Ukraine sometime around 1100 BCE. Little is known of them, although when they were pushed out of their steppe home-

land by new invaders from the east, they moved southward and settled in Crimea. The migratory pattern followed by the Cimmerians was to be repeated subsequently by other nomadic groups who were forced to leave the steppes of Ukraine and who found in Crimea their final place of refuge until being absorbed by the local population.

When remnants of the Cimmerians reached Crimea sometime in the seventh century BCE, they encountered a people already living there, who were known in ancient written sources as the Taurians (Tauricae). The Taurians were a tribal group of unknown origin, who, at least from the first millennium BCE, lived in the mountainous zone of the Crimea where they engaged in animal husbandry, some agriculture, and fishing along the coasts. Not only are the Taurians considered by some authors the aboriginal, or first settlers in Crimea, their very name was adopted by ancient Greek writers as a geographic term for the peninsula, which they called Taurica. That name lived on into the modern era, and as late as the early twentieth century the Russian imperial province, which

---

◀ *Entryway to the cave-town Kirk Yer/Chufut-Kale.*

Scythian sphere of influence, 550 BCE - 200 CE

Bosporan Kingdom, 5th - 3rd centuries BCE

■ Scythian fortified settlement

• Greek settlement

included within its boundaries Crimea, was called Taurica—Taurida.

Ancient authors became aware of Crimea/Taurica, because Greek sailors in the seventh century BCE began to ply the well established trade routes from the Aegean to the Black Seas. By the sixth century BCE, Greek city-states, in particular Miletus (in present-day south-western Turkey) and Megara (near Athens in modern-day Greece) encouraged settlers, whether motivated by economic or political reasons, to colonize the northern shores of the Black Sea. The result was that by the sixth century BCE several prosperous Greek cities came into being along the shores of the Black Sea, the Straits of Kerch, and the Sea of Azov. Among the first major settlements were Tiras at the mouth of the Dniester River and Olbia at the mouth of the Southern Buh River, followed by Chersonesus, Theodosia, and Panticapaeum (Bospor) along the coasts of the Crimean Peninsula from its southwestern tip to the Straits of Kerch at its eastern end.

Like the Greek homeland along both shores of the Aegean Sea, the Greek colonies along the northern Black Sea coast initially remained independent of each other, although they were economically and politically linked to the city-state which founded them, in particular Miletus and Megara. There were also periods when the Black Sea colonies were completely independent, or when they united into federations or states.

The most important of these federations came into being about 480 BCE,

Crimean dolmen, 6th-5th century BCE—Taurian stone burial vault on Mt. Kishka near Simeyiz.

when the Greek cities near the Straits of Kerch were drawn together under the leadership of Panticapaeum into what became known as the Bosporan Kingdom. Eventually, the Bosporan Kingdom became independent of the Aegean Greek homeland, and under its dynamic king Levkon I (reigned ca. 389-348 BCE) it came to control lands on the western (Kerch peninsula) and eastern (Taman peninsula) sides of the Straits of Kerch, as well as steppelands (Kuban) east of the Sea of Azov. Until the end of the second century BCE, the Bosporan Kingdom flourished as a center of grain trading, fishing, wine making, and small-scale artisan craftsmanship, especially metalworking. Then it entered a period of political instability until it was annexed (110 BCE) by Pontus, or the Pontic Kingdom, which was based along the southern shores of the Black Sea under the powerful ruler Mithradates VI Eupator (reigned 113-63 BCE). Toward

The acropolis of Panticapeum, 2nd century BCE, reconstruction

Image of Parthenos (the Virgin), supreme Taurian deity on a coin of Chersonesus.

Mithradates VI (Eupator, ca 131-63 BCE), king of Pontus and Bosporan Kingdom in Crimea.

the end of his reign, Mithradates made Panticapeum the center of his ongoing struggle with the Roman republic. After his death, the Bosporan Kingdom together with other Hellenic cities around the Black Sea came under the control of Rome.

About the same time that the first Greek sailors and settlers reached the southern shores of Crimea, nomadic tribes from the east, who were of Iranic origin and known as Scythians, arrived in the steppes of Ukraine. The Scythians displaced the Cimmerians and soon came to rule the inhabitants of much of present-day Ukraine from the lower Don River to the Danubian delta. It was during the nearly four centuries between 600 to 250 BCE that the Greek cities along the Black Sea littoral, including the southern Crimea and Bosporan Kingdom, developed a symbiotic relationship with the Scythian hinterland to the north. The three components com-

prising that relationship were: (1) the Scythian-controlled Ukrainian steppe; (2) the Black Sea Greek cities; and (3) the Greek city-states along the shores of the Aegean Sea.

These three territorial components were interlinked by economic interests. Bread and fish were the staple foods of ancient Greece, and the increasing demand for these products was met by markets in Crimea and other northern

Queen Dynamis, granddaughter of Mithradates VI, first ruler (44-14 BCE) of the Bosporan Kingdom appointed by Rome.

Neapolis, capital of Scythia Minor, 2nd century BCE,
drawing by B. V. Kondratskyi based on a reconstruction by T. M. Vysotska.

Black Sea Greek coastal cities. And from where did the coastal cities obtain these food products? From Ukrainian steppe lands, which already in ancient times had a reputation for their natural wealth.

The Scythians extracted grain and fish from the sedentary inhabitants of Ukraine who were under their control, and then traded these commodities in the Black Sea coastal cities along with cattle, hides, furs, wax, honey, and slaves, also derived from the Ukrainian steppe hinterland. These products brought a lucrative profit to Crimea's Scythian overlords after being sent southward to Aegean Greece. In return, the Scythians bought from the Greeks textiles, wines, olive oil, art works, and other luxury items to satisfy their opulent tastes. Among those luxury items were what subsequently came to be known as "Scythian Gold." These were objects of finely wrought jewellery and other ornamental items, which depicted hunted animals and warriors, subjects that responded to the tastes of the Scythian military elite. It seems likely that the golden objects were not produced by the nomadic Scythians themselves, but rather by Greek and other artisans working in the coastal cities of Crimea and other northern Black Sea settlements.

The Scythians brought a period of peace and stability to Crimea and the southern Ukrainian steppelands which lasted for about five-hundred years and which has come to be known as the *Pax Scythica*, or Scythian Peace; that is, general stability in international affairs made possible because of Scythian military strength and accompanying social order. It would be some time before such long-term stability would come again to the region. This is because around 250 BCE, another nomadic people from the east, the Sarmatians, pushed their way into the Ukrainian steppe. Like the Scythians, the Sarmatians were Iranian-speaking warrior horsemen, who headed a loose federation of several related tribes, among which the most prominent were the Roxolani and Alans. Since

Sarmatian women usually fought alongside males, the ancient Greeks connected the Sarmatians with the Amazons. These were the famed female warriors of Greek mythology, who allegedly left their original homeland in Asia Minor (present-day Turkey), settled on the eastern shores of the Sea of Azov, and whose descendants were believed to be the Sarmatians.

At least during the first two centuries of the Sarmatian presence, from 250 to 50 BCE, the relative stability and resultant economic prosperity that had previously existed between the Scythian hinterland and the Greek cities of

Fortified tower at Scythian Neapolis on Keremchik hill in modern-day Simferopol.

the coast was disrupted. Pressed by the Sarmatians in the steppe, the Scythian leaders and their military elite fled to Crimea. Their realm was now limited to the lowlands plains of western Crimea and a small area along the banks of the lower Dnieper River. This entity was known to the classical world as Scythia Minor (Inner Scythia) with its fortified administrative center at Neapolis (the New City). Built toward the end of the second century BCE atop a large mound (within present-day Simferopol), Neapolis and Scythia Minor reached the height of their power under King Skilur (reigned ca. 125-113 BCE). Initially, the rulers based in Neapolis tried to continue the traditional Scythian practice of exacting tribute from the Greek cities along the coast. But because they no longer controlled the resources of the Ukrainian steppes, they had little to give the Greeks in return. The result was frequent conflict between the Scythians north of the Crimean Mountains and the Greek cities along the coast and the Bosporan Kingdom along the Straits of Kerch.

This era of instability, which affected not only the Sarmatian-controlled hinterland but also the Black Sea cities, eventually came to an end along the coastal region. Following its victories over Mithradates VI and his death in 63 BCE, Rome (still a republic about to become an empire) succeeded in extending its sphere of influence over the independent Black Sea Greek cities as well as over those within the Bosporan Kingdom. With the presence of Roman

The cave-town of Kirk Yer/Chufut-Kale as it appears today.

legions and administrators in the region, peace and stability were restored. The *Pax Romana*, the new social order imposed by Roman military might, not only reduced the friction between the Scythians and the Greeks of Crimea, it also convinced the Sarmatian tribes in the Ukrainian hinterland of the advantages of some kind of cooperation with the Roman world. Reacting to the stabilizing presence of the Romans, some tribes within the Sarmatian federation, in particular the Alans, renewed the Scythian tradition of trade with the Greco-Roman cities along the coast.

The Alans were a Sarmatian tribal group originally based in the lowlands between the Caucasus Mountains and the Sea of Azov. Sometime toward the end of the second century CE, they expanded westward into Crimea. Some settled in the mountainous region, where they were among the first inhabitants in the hilltop town of Kirk Yer (Tatar: Qirq Yer; later Chufut-Kale). Others preferred the Black Sea coastal region. In their new Crimean homeland, the nomadic Alans switched to a sedentary lifestyle and engaged in agriculture, cattle-breeding, and handicrafts. Further adapting to their new environment in Crimea, the Alans adopted Christianity. This was one of the reasons they were able to assimilate easily with other Christian inhabitants and become part of a Greek-Scythian-Sarmatian hybrid

GOTHIC AND BYZANTINE CRIMEA, ca. 650

MAP 3

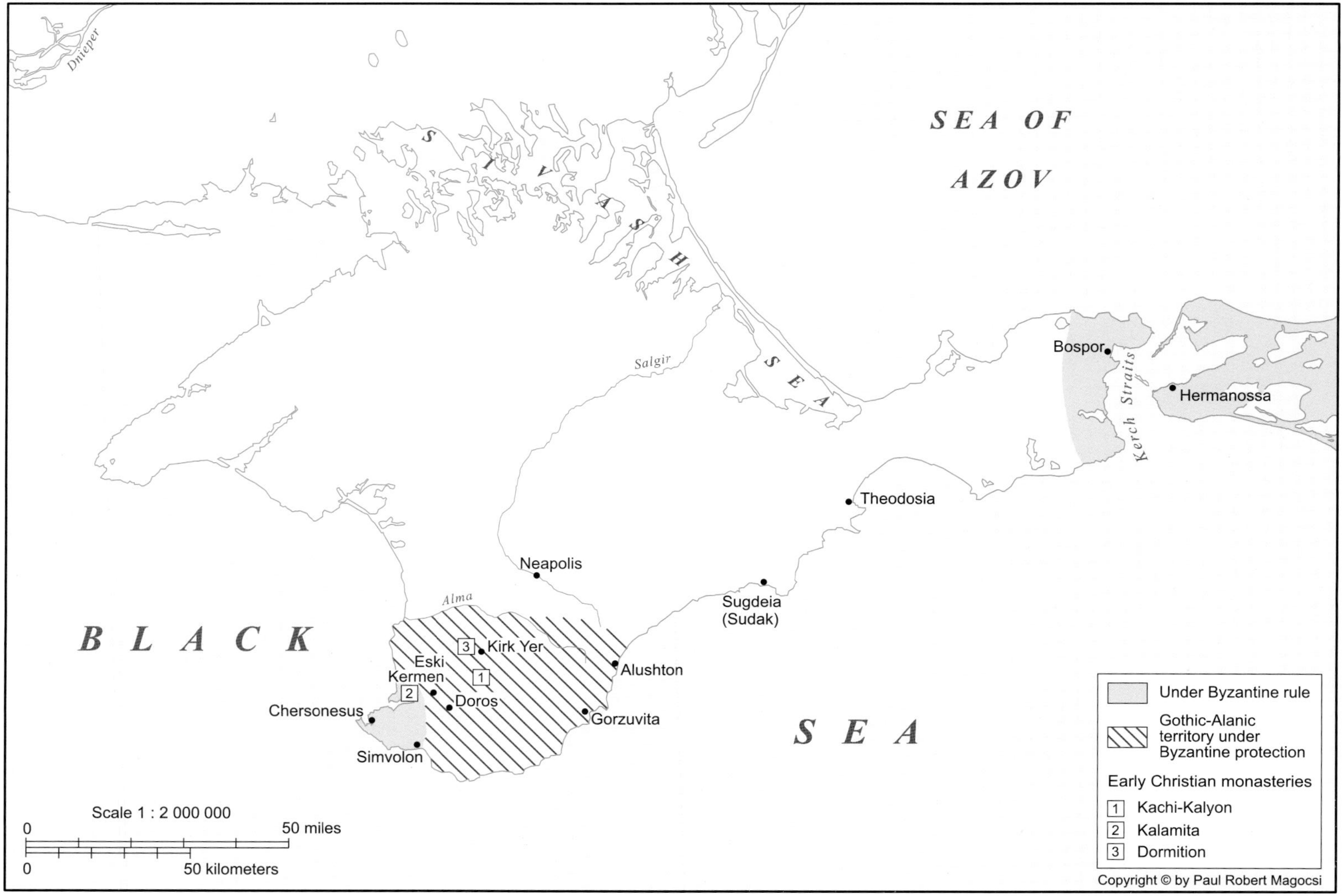
Dnieper
SEA OF AZOV
SIVASH SEA
Salgir
Alma
Bospor
Hermanossa
Kerch Straits
Theodosia
Neapolis
Sugdeia
(Sudak)
Kirk Yer
Eski
Kermen
Doros
Chersonesus
Simvolon
Alushton
Gorzuvita
BLACK SEA
Scale 1 : 2 000 000
0
50 miles
0
50 kilometers
Under Byzantine rule
Gothic-Alanic territory under Byzantine protection
Early Christian monasteries
1 Kachi-Kalyon
2 Kalamita
3 Dormition
Copyright © by Paul Robert Magocsi

civilization which evolved in Crimea and the Bosporan Kingdom under the protection of the Roman Empire. The resultant trade and commerce between the steppe hinterland and the Mediterranean world of Rome brought a renewed prosperity to Crimea and the Bosporan Kingdom that characterized the first two centuries of the common era.

The third century CE, however, ushered in another era of instability. For the next four centuries, the steppelands of Ukraine and southern Russia were to be subjected to invasions by several new nomadic warrior tribes who were bent on destruction and plunder of the classical world as represented by the Crimean and Bosporan Black Sea coastal cities. With few exceptions, the nomads were not interested—as the Scythians and eventually the Sarmatians had been before them—in settling down and exploiting by peaceful means the symbiotic relationship between Ukraine's steppe hinterland and Crimea's coastal cities.

The four centuries of strife between 250 and 650 CE began not with the arrival of nomads from Central Asia, but rather with the incursion of Germanic tribes known as Goths from northern Europe. Believed to have originated from what is today southern Sweden, the Goths had by 50 BCE moved to the southern shores of the Baltic Sea (i.e., modern-day Poland). It was from there that toward the end of the second century CE they moved southward into Ukraine. They broke the Sarmatian dominance of the steppe hinterland and came into contact with the Roman world along the northern shores of the Black Sea. The Goths had by this time split into two branches: those tribes that moved westward into the Roman Empire came to be known as Visigoths; those that remained in Ukraine became known as Ostrogoths, or East Goths. After 250 CE, Ostrogoths captured Olbia and Tiras from the Romans, with the result that during the following century the Greco-Roman coastal cities along the northern shores of the Black Sea, as well as Scythian Neapolis and the Bosporan Kingdom in Crimea, were drawn along with the southern Ukrainian steppe hinterland into the sphere of the Ostrogothic Kingdom.

Ostrogothic rule in southern Ukraine and Crimea reached its apogee under King Ermanaric (reigned 350-375). Gothic hegemony proved to be short-lived, however, because already toward the end of Ermanaric's reign (ca. 370) a new nomadic people, this time from Central Asia, arrived in the steppes of Ukraine. These were the Huns, who easily subjected the Ostrogoths and for about a century dominated the entire steppe region from the Caspian Sea to the heart of Europe. The Huns moved rapidly westward and forced many of the Ostrogoths to join their military ranks as they attacked the Roman Empire. Those Ostrogoths who were not taken westward by the Huns remained in Crimea, where they found refuge in the mountainous back country away from the more vulnerable coast.

The Crimean Goths, as they came to be known, were anxious to maintain

Chersonesus. Ancient Greek theater, mid-3rd century BCE.

good relations with what by then had became the Eastern Roman, or Byzantine Empire with its new imperial capital founded in the 330s at Constantinople (modern-day Istanbul). The "New Rome" was named for its founder, Constantine I, the emperor who made Christianity the official religion of the realm. Hence, Constantinople became the center of the Christian Church of the Eastern, or Byzantine rite.

The center of the East Roman/ Byzantine administration in Crimea was the port city of Chersonesus (on the western edge of present-day Sevastopol), which during sixth-century reign of Emperor Justinian I was strengthened with fortifications, as were other towns along the coast: Simvolon (present-day Balaklava), Alushton (present-day Alushta), Gorzuvita (present-day Hurzuf), and Bospor (present-day Kerch). Anxious to protect the coastal cities against the ever pres-

ent threat of attacks by nomadic tribesmen from the north, Byzantine engineers were sent to assist the Crimean Goths and Alans in fortifying several "cave towns" on the top of mountain cliffs and promontories, which in some cases rose up to 200 meters (600 feet) above the surrounding valleys. Despite the popular designation given to them, the inhabitants of these naturally fortified sites did not live in caves but rather in structures built from wood and stone on the top of the caves (usually used for storage or as a part of the defense system) and along the table-top promontories that in some cases covered tens of acres of territory. Among the largest of the Crimean hill-top "cave towns" were Mangup, Kirk Yer, and Eski Kermen located in the hinterland northeast of Chersonesus. The Crimean Gothic center was a place called Doros/Dory, most likely at what later became known as

Mangup, located about halfway between Chersonesus and the Scythian center at Neapolis.

In the course of the fourth century, the Ostrogoths accepted Christianity according to the Eastern Orthodox Byzantine rite, although they adopted so-called Arian views regarding the nature of Jesus Christ, which differed from church doctrine and which were eventually declared heretical. More important was the fact that the acceptance of Christianity cemented Crimean Gothic relations with the East Roman/Byzantine Empire. At the outset of the fifth century (ca. 400 CE), the head of the church in Constantinople appointed a bishop for Crimea's Eparchy/Diocese of Gothia, whose seat was in the Gothic center of Doros. Therefore, the Crimean Goths, as well as the peninsula's Alans,

became through their Christian faith part of the Byzantine political and cultural sphere. For the next five centuries the Alano-Gothic Christians functioned as a protective shield for the Greco-Byzantine coastal cities against further invasions by nomads from the north.

The coastal cities, as centers of trade, commerce, and Byzantine Orthodox Christian culture, remained attractive to new waves of Greek settlement. This was especially the case in the seventh and eighth centuries, when the iconoclast controversy in Byzantium (opposition to the imperial ban on images in churches) forced religious and political dissidents to seek refuge in the empire's peripheral regions such as Crimea. Among the newcomers to Crimea from the heart of the Byzantine Empire were religious zealots and protectors of vener-

Chersonesus. Remnants of a 6th-century Christian basilica uncovered by archeologists in 1935.

21

able icons, who founded several Orthodox monasteries and hermitages (sketes) to practice the "true" faith without interference from the state. Often built in inaccessible places, including on the sites of the mountain-top "cave cities" and along the sheer faces of cliffs, the best known monasteries were at Kachi-Kalyon, Kalamita/Inkerman, and the Dormition (Uspenskyi) near Kirk Yer and what is present-day Bakhchysaray.

While Crimea was within the political and cultural sphere of Orthodox Christianity, the steppe hinterland in southern Ukraine continued to experience periodic incursions by a whole host of mostly Turkic-speaking nomadic peoples from the east: Utigurs, Avars, Bulgars, Khazars, Magyars, Pechenegs, and Kipchaks. Some passed quickly through the steppe on their way west-

The Baptism of the Prince St. Volodymyr, *painting (1890) by Viktor Vasnetsov.*

ward toward Europe; others, like the Khazars, set up more permanent state-like structures that provided a degree of peace and stability to the steppe. In this regard, the Khazars were most successful, and during the eighth century they incorporated the Crimean steppe zone and eventually much of the coastal region into their state. Sudak became the center of Khazar rule, and, along with military garrisons, Turkic-speaking settlers took up permanent residence especially in eastern Crimea.

Much farther north beyond the open steppes, a new element made its appearance in eastern Europe. These were the Rus', a varied assortment of warriors, traders, and adventurers from the Baltic region of Scandinavia, whose eastward expeditions reached the Black Sea and Azov region already in the eighth century. Sometime in the 850s, the Rus' together with several East Slavic tribal groups under their hegemony created a state structure that was eventually based in Kyiv and that henceforth came to be known as Kievan Rus'. Toward the end of the tenth century, a Rus' principality was established at Tmutorokhan on the eastern shores of the Straits of Kerch. Although such a location allowed for easy access and direct contact with Crimea, there is no indication that East Slavs settled the peninsula in any large numbers.

On the other hand, the Rus' looked to Crimea as a source for an important commodity in medieval society—salt. Crimea became even more important on what might be called the ideological front. Sometime in the 980s, the senior,

Kerch. Church of John the Baptist, Byzantine architecture from the late ninth-early 10th century.

or grand prince of Kyiv, Volodymyr/ Vladimir ("the Great," r. 980-1015), decided to adopt Christianity as the official religion of what had until then been the pagan Rus' state. Ever since their arrival in eastern Europe, the Rus' were drawn to the Byzantine world and the riches of its capital, Constantinople. Volodymyr hoped to enhance the Rus'-Byzantine relationship by providing military assistance to the emperor and, after promising to convert to Christianity according to the Eastern Orthodox Byzantine rite, receive in return the hand of the emperor's sister in marriage. Negotiations on these matters took place in 987 in Chersonesus, Byzantium's administrative capital in Crimea. Two years later, Chersonesus was also the alleged site of Volodymyr's conversion and marriage. Henceforth, the Rus' became part of the larger Byzantine Orthodox cultural sphere, with the result that since that time Crimea has held a special place in the hearts and minds of culturally conscious Orthodox Russians, Belarusans, and Ukrainians. In other words, Crimea remains intimately connected with the most important spiritual and cultural event in the history of those three peoples—the Christianization of Rus'.

Chapter 3

The Kipchaks, Mongols, Tatars, and Italianate Crimea

Aside from their connection with Byzantine Christian Crimea, the Rus' also had a decisive impact on the steppe region. In the 960s, the Rus' prince Sviatoslav destroyed the political centers of the Khazar Kaganate which for two centuries had controlled much of the steppe region north of the Caucasus from the Caspian Sea in the east to the Don River and beyond in the west. In the absence of the Khazar Kaganate, the steppelands witnessed increasing conflict among existing and newly arrived Turkic tribal groups from Central Asia. Among these were the Pechenegs, Torks, and Berendei, who in the tenth and most of the eleventh centuries dominated southern Ukraine, and from there they periodically made their way to the Crimean peninsula. Among the Turkic nomads from the east who managed to remain for an even longer time were the Kipchaks.

Known by several names—including Polovtsians (*polovtsi*) in Slavic sources and Cumans (*Comani*) and Kuns in Greek and western European sources—the Kipchaks (Turkic: *Qipçaq*) reached southern Ukraine in the mid-eleventh century. For the next two centuries they controlled trade routes through the open steppe and created a rudimentary state-like formation called Desht-i-Qipçaq—Steppe of the Kipchaks. Included within their sphere of control was the steppe zone of Crimea. Despite their military prowess as agile armed horsemen, some Kipchak tribal leaders preferred, when possible, to reach mutually beneficial arrangements with their neighbors. Among these were the Rus', with whom the Kipchaks experienced both fierce conflict as well as periods of peace and even close cooperation which took the form of joint military campaigns and marriage alliances with Rus' princes.

The Kipchaks established economic ties with Byzantium through the empire's ports in Crimea, such as Yalta and most especially Sudak. From the coastal ports Byzantine products were transported across Crimea's mountains and then placed on caravans that travelled northward through the Kipchak steppe to Kievan Rus', reaching markets in Kyiv and other cities as far as Novgorod. Kipchak-Rus' relations were especially good at the outset of the thirteenth century,

◀ *Balbal, a Polovstian gravestone, 11th-12th century.*

MAP 4

THE GOLDEN HORDE, ca. 1300

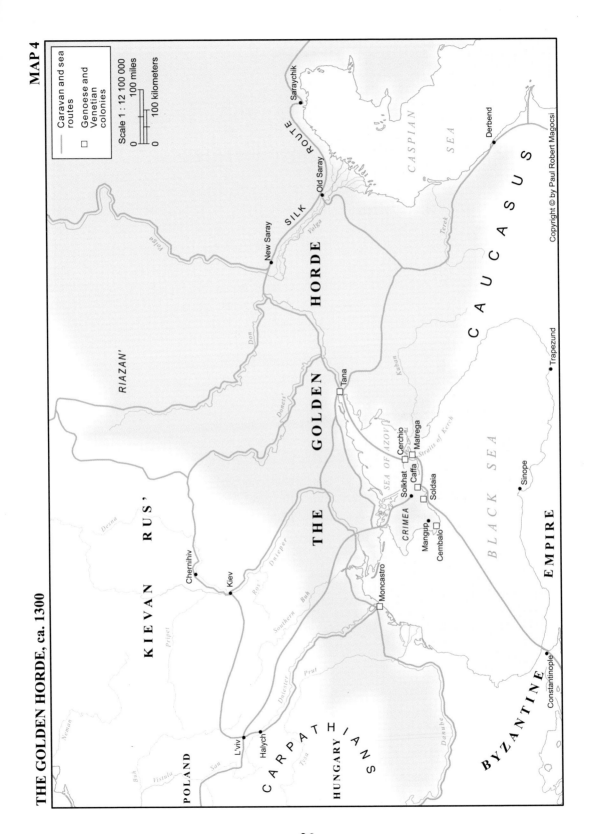

Caravan and sea routes

☐ Genoese and Venetian colonies

Scale 1 : 12 100 000

0   100 miles

0   100 kilometers

Copyright © by Paul Robert Magocsi

CASPIAN SEA

Saraychik

Derbend

Old Saray

New Saray

SILK ROUTE

Volga

Volga

Terek

THE GOLDEN HORDE

Don

Donets'

Kuban

RIAZAN'

CAUCASUS

Trapezund

Tana

SEA OF AZOV

Straits of Kerch

Cerchio

Matrega

Solkhat

Caffa

Soldaia

CRIMEA

Mangup

Cembalo

Sinope

BLACK SEA

KIEVAN RUS'

Desna

Chernihiv

Kiev

Dnieper

Ros'

Moncastro

Southern Buh

BYZANTINE EMPIRE

Constantinople

Pripet

Noman

Buh

Vistula

San

L'viv

Halych

Dniester

Prut

Tisa

Danube

POLAND

CARPATHIANS

HUNGARY

which could be considered a relatively stable period in the history of Ukraine's steppe hinterland. The Kipchak-Rus' détente and the stability that it created was, however, to come to an unexpected and brutal end. The reason was the arrival of yet another warrior group from the east—the Mongols.

Originating in the highland steppes of Mongolia between China and Siberia, the Mongol and several neighboring Turkic tribes were united in 1206 under a local chief named Temujin. Following his success, Temujin adopted the epithet Chinggis (literally: the severe one), and has come to be known in history as Chinggis Khan. Under Chinggis's direction and during the two decades until his death in 1227, the Mongol armies conquered a vast territory stretching from China and Manchuria on the Pacific coast in the far east and continuing through the steppes and plateaus of Central Asia and northern Persia as far as the Caspian Sea.

Although the Great Khan's armies were led by a Mongol elite, the vast majority of soldiers were actually Tatars (tribal groups originally from the Mongolo-Chinese borderland) and Turkic peoples that the Mongols picked up during their conquests. The extensive territory brought under Mongol rule ushered in a new political order and era of prosperity that some writers, recalling earlier periods of international stability, refer to as the *Pax Mongolica*.

While Chinggis Khan was still alive, in 1222 a Mongol expeditionary force was dispatched westward and be-yond the Caspian Sea into the lands of the Kipchaks. The Mongol force first passed through Crimea as far as the coast, where it attacked and pillaged the port of Sudak. Frightened by this new threat from the east, the Kipchaks turned to their allies in Kievan Rus'. The result was the formation of a joint Rus'-Kipchak force, which in 1223 set out to stop the invaders. It was, however, completely routed after three days of battle near the Kalka River just north of the Sea of Azov. Undeterred, the Mongol expedition continued toward the southern border of Kievan Rus', but then suddenly turned eastward and returned to Mongolia.

With the knowledge gained by the expeditionary force from its encounter with the Kipchaks and the Rus', the Mongols returned fifteen years later. This time they came with a massive military force estimated at between 120,000 and 140,000 troops under the supreme

Tatar archer, anonymous Chinese painting from the 15th century.

27

Staryi Krym/Eski Kirim. Remnants of the medrese *(theological college)
and 14th-century mosque of Özbeg, the Mongol Khan of the Golden Horde.*

command of Chinggis Khan's grandson, Khan Batu. The Mongol armies first entered the northeastern Rus' principalities of Murom-Riazan and Vladimir-Suzdal, which they easily conquered during the winter of 1237-1238. Then they decided to move southward and rest for the next two and a half years on the Steppe of the Kipchaks. It was during this time that the Kipchak polity came to an end. Some Kipchaks were pressed into Mongol service; others sought refuge among the Rus'; still others fled westward, eventually settling in Hungary. Those who managed to remain in the Ukrainian and Crimean steppelands integrated with the Mongol rulers and their Tatar and Turkic subordinates.

At the end of 1240, the Mongols relaunched their campaign toward Europe. They first entered southern Rus', capturing the city of Kyiv (December 1240), after which the Mongols moved rapidly westward through Galicia and further on into Poland and Hungary. Eventually, the various Mongol armies converged on Hungary, where they spent the winter of 1241-1242 in the steppe-like regions of that country. When, in the spring of 1242, Batu learned of the death of the Great Khan of Mongolia, he set off with his entire armed force to return home. Along the way, however, he established a Mongol administrative outpost along the lower Volga River at a place called Saray, where Batu shortly returned to become the first ruling khan (r. 1242-1256).

Under Batu, Saray soon developed into a powerful administrative and commercial center from which the Mongols were to rule their new conquests in eastern Europe. Their new political entity, which was based in the lower Volga River valley, encompassed the entire steppe region north of the Black, Caspian, and Aral seas from the upper reaches of the Ob River in Siberia to the Danube River in southeastern Europe. This vast land mass included all of modern-day Kazakhstan, Ukraine (with Crimea), and much of central and southern Russia from Kazan on the upper Volga River to the Caucasus Mountains. As the westernmost component (*ulus*) of the Mongol Empire, it was called the Kipchak Khanate or, in western and Muscovite sources, the Golden Horde.

The Mongols were always small in number and easily susceptible to assimilation into the cultures and traditions of the numerous peoples they ruled. A momentous development in this regard occurred in the 1330s, when the Mongol elite, headed by Khan Özbeg (r. 1313-1342), adopted Islam as the official religion of the Golden Horde. Gradually, that religion was also adopted by the Turkic Kipchaks with whom the Mongols intermarried. For some reason that still remains unclear, the name Tatar was adopted by—and also used by outsiders to describe—all the inhabitants of the Golden Horde, both its Mongol ruling elite and its subordinate Turkic-speaking tribal clans.

About the same time that the Mongols were changing the political configuration of the entire steppe hinterland north of the Black Sea, Crimea's mountainous and coastal zones were also going through a major transformation. In short, the hegemony of Byzantium in these regions was coming to an end and was about to be replaced by an unexpected source—Italianate merchant states from Mediterranean Europe.

In 1204, Crusaders from western Europe on their way to recover the Christian Holy Land in Palestine were diverted from their original goal and went instead to Constantinople, the capital of the Byzantine Empire. Instead of uniting against their common enemy, the

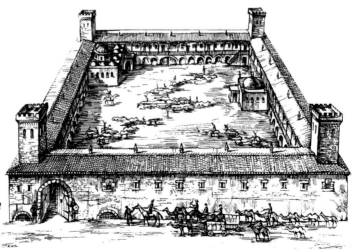

Bilohirsk/Karasubazar. Reconstruction of the 14th-century Stone Palace/Tash-Khan caravansary, an inn for caravans arriving in Crimea, reconstruction by Riza Abduzhemilev.

Sudak/Soldaia. Genoese fortress (1365-1475).

Abbasid Muslim state, which at the time controlled the Holy Land, the Western Roman Catholic Christians fought against what were described as "schismatic" Eastern Orthodox Christians. Constantinople was sacked, the emperor of Byzantium was driven into exile, and a western Latin Empire headed by Roman Catholic military adventurers from Europe was established in the heart of the Orthodox Christian East.

The sacking of Constantinople by Western Roman Catholic Christian forces impacted Crimea in two ways. Along the coast, Byzantine rule collapsed and was replaced by new forces from the south and west. Already in the early 1220s, the Seljuk Turks expanded their influence from Anatolia to the northern shores of the Black Sea, where they placed under their control the port of Sudak. Although their administrative presence in Crimea was short lived, the close relations of the Seljuks with the Golden Horde resulted in an influx of

Turkic (Oğuz) settlers from Anatolia to the Crimean steppelands, especially during the second half of the thirteenth century. About the same time, Italianate merchants from the Republic of Venice/Venetia and the city-state of Genoa came and settled in ports along the coast.

It was the Golden Horde, however, which remained the dominant power in the region and made Crimea part of its domain. The Mongol rulers did not hesitate to enforce their authority in the peninsula by demanding an annual tribute and taxes from the Italianate coastal cities. Mongol authority was embodied in a governor who was resident in the town of Solkhat/Krym (Turkic: Kirim/Eski-Kirim), a commercial and Islamic cultural center in the eastern part of the peninsula located north of Sudak beyond the coastal cliffs and on the edge of the lowland steppe.

As part of the *Pax Mongolica*, or Mongol political order, Crimea was drawn into the network of caravan routes that began in China and moved westward across the vast expanse of the steppelands of Central Asia. The main trunk of this trading network was the famed Silk Route. At its western end, it took after 1261 an alternative route that passed north of the Caspian Sea to Saray, and from there farther southwestward across the Sea of Azov to Crimea's Black Sea ports. The silk, spices, and other lucrative land goods were then loaded onto ships bound for Constantinople and Mediterranean Europe.

The Black Sea trading nexus, which dated back to ancient times, was after 1261 promoted by the rulers of Golden Horde. Crimea's coastal cities were once again revived, although this time under the leadership of Italian merchants from Venice and, eventually, Genoa. In the 1280s, the Mongols allowed the Genoese to build on the site of the ancient Greek town of Theodosia several maritime warehouses around which developed the port city of Caffa. Within a few decades, Genoese and, to a lesser degree, Venetian influence spread throughout the region, with the result that Crimea's Byzantine port cities became known to the outside world by their Italian names: Caffa (modern-day Feodosiya), Soldaia (Sudak), Lupico (Alupka), Cembalo (Balaklava), and Cerchio (Kerch). All these port cities became not only markets for international trade, but also centers of local manufacturing and crafts.

The main center for the Caspian-Black-Mediterranean Sea trading network was Genoese-controlled Caffa. The city grew rapidly, so that by the last decades of Genoese rule in the second half of the fifteenth century it had over 70,000 inhabitants. Like other cities along the Crimean coast, Caffa was inhabited by a heterogeneous mix of Byzantine Greeks, Slavs, Vlachs, Tatars, and Jews (both Turkic-speaking Krimchaks and the non-Talmudic sect known as Karaim/Karaites), among others. Among those others were Armenians, who since the eleventh century had been arriving in Crimea as refugees from their Caucasus homeland that had been conquered by the Seljuk Turks. So large was their immigration that by the fifteenth century two-thirds of Caffa's huge pop-

Genoese merchants in Caffa. *14th-century manuscript book illustration.*

ulation consisted of Armenians, with the result that some sources from the period refer to the entire Crimean peninsula as "Armenia Maritime" or "Armenia Magna."

Overseeing all of Caffa's inhabitants was an administration in the hands of about a thousand Genoese, whose trading companies (factories) and bankers maintained good relations with the Byzantine Empire (which was restored in 1261) while at the same time being directly linked to the economy of their homeland city of Genoa. While Caffa's main local industry was shipbuilding, the city's greatest wealth came from its control of the international trade in silks and spices from Central Asia as well as fish, grains, hides, and slaves from the Mongol-controlled steppe hinterland. Processed in Crimea, these material and human goods were brought on Genoese or Venetian ships to the Byzantine Empire and further on across the Mediterranean Sea to the ports of southern Europe.

The early phase of the Italianate presence along the southern Crimean coast was marked by military conflict between the Genoese and Venetian rivals and by disagreement with the Mongol overlords, conflicts which were eventually resolved by negotiated settlements. Although the Genoese eventually eliminated their Venetian rivals, their control of the coastal regions and its dominance

Feodosiya/Caffa. St. Sarkis/Sergey Armenian Church, 14th century.
Alongside is the burial place of the renowned Crimea-born painter of Armenian
origin Ivan Aivazovskyi/Ovanes Aivazian.

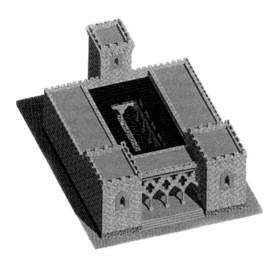

*Mangup. Palace of the Princes
of Theodoro, 14th century,
reconstruction by N. Menchinskaya
and Tatyana Fadeeva.*

over maritime trade was to be challenged yet by another force. In the second half of the fourteenth century, Greek refugees fleeing Latin rule in Byzantium created a Christian principality called Theodoro in the mountainous highlands behind the coastal region. This was an area which from the fifth to tenth centuries was controlled by descendents of Crimean Goths and Alans, who in the interim had become Hellenized; that is, assimilated to Byzantine Christian culture and the Greek language. Because the Byzantine church jurisdiction set up in the area was called the archeparchy and later Metropolitanate of Gothia, Theodoro was also referred to in some sources as the Principality of Go-

thia. From the 1360s, Theodoro's capital was at Mangup, the largely inaccessible mountain-top town and former Gothic center of Doros located about halfway between Bakhchysarai and the Black Sea coast (see Map 6). The Theodoro principality was inhabited by a heterogeneous mix of peoples who, aside from Hellenized Goths and Alans, included Byzantine Greeks, Slavs, Tatars, Kipchaks, and Karaites.

From their fortified center at Mangup, the princes of Theodoro, who were mostly Byzantine Greeks, in the course of the fifteenth century expanded their realm down to the Crimean coast, where in the far southwest they developed the port of Avlita and, immediately above it on the cliffs, constructed the fortress of Kalamita (today Inkerman). During the reign of Prince Aleksei (ca. 1405-1455), the Theodorites captured several port cities from the Genoese, thereby expanding their rule along the Black Sea coast from Cembalo (Balaklava) eastward to Alushta. In essence, from the late thirteenth to the late fifteenth century, the classic symbiotic relationship between the steppe hinterland and Crimea's coastal cities was reestablished. This era of stability in the Crimea was the result of a modus vivendi between three forces: the Mongolo-Tatar Golden Horde, the Italianate Genoese, and the Byzantine-Greek principality of Mangup-Theodoro.

Chapter 4

The Crimean Khanate

Despite its historic relationship to the powerful Mongol Empire of Chinggis Khan, the Golden Horde was not invincible. Already in the second half of the fourteenth century it entered an extended period of decline, which was the result of internal conflicts among rival contenders for the khan's throne that was only made worse by foreign invasions, whether from the north by the Grand Duchy of Lithuania, or from the east by a claimant to the universal Mongol heritage, Timur (Tamerlane). The Golden Horde managed to survive these threats, although in the course of the fifteenth century its territorial integrity disintegrated and it was eventually replaced by three distinct—and rival— Tatar political entities. Two of these entities came into existence already during the 1440s in peripheral regions of the Golden Horde: the Kazan Khanate along the middle Volga River, and the Crimean Khanate in the Crimean Peninsula and areas north of the Sea of Azov. These two entities claimed authority over all the lands that had once belonged to the Golden Horde, al- though their claims were challenged by two increasingly powerful neighbors to the north: the Grand Duchy of Lithuania and the Tsardom of Muscovy.

The Golden Horde, though territorially reduced in size, managed to survive for another half century in its heartland between the Volga and Kuban Rivers. In 1502, however, the Golden Horde ceased to exist, with its remaining territory becoming the basis of the third rival Tatar successor state, the Astrakhan Khanate. Each of the three khanates continued the Mongol practice of exacting tribute from those states that ruled lands formerly part of Kievan Rus'. The Kazan and Astrakhan khanates received payments from Muscovy; the Crimean Khanate from Muscovy and also from Lithuania and Poland. The three Tatar states became formidable powers in their own right. Hence, much of the early history of both Lithuania and Muscovy was marked by efforts to rid themselves of what was considered the odious and humiliating heritage of the Golden Horde's "Tatar yoke" as maintained by the Kazan, Astrakhan, and Crimean khanates.

◀ *Bakhchysaray. Palace of the Khans: the Great Khan Mosque of Sahib Giray, built in the 16th century, reconstructed in the 18th century.*

MAP 5

SUCCESSOR STATES OF THE GOLDEN HORDE, ca. 1520

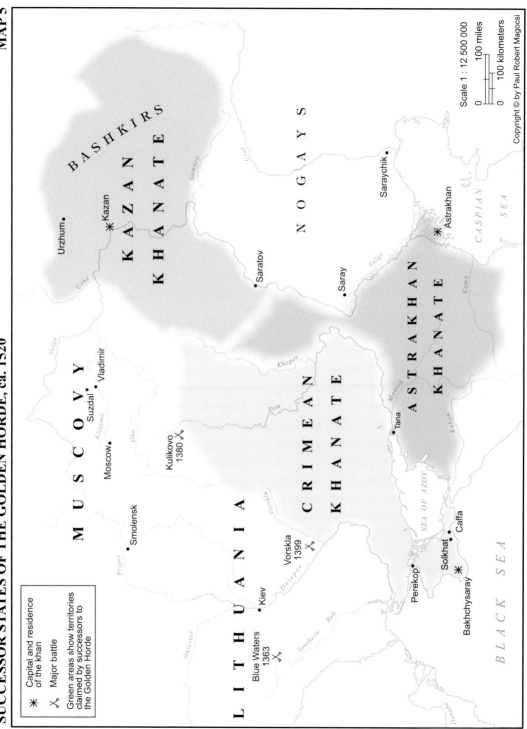

Capital and residence
of the khan

Major battle

Green areas show territories
claimed by successors to
the Golden Horde

B A S H K I R S

KAZAN KHANATE

K A Z A N   K H A N A T E

Urzhum

Kazan

N O G A Y S

Saraychik

Astrakhan

CASPIAN   SEA

MUSCOVY

M U S C O V Y

Vladimir

Suzdal

Moscow

Smolensk

Kulikovo
1380

Saratov

Saray

ASTRAKHAN KHANATE

A S T R A K H A N   K H A N A T E

Tana

CRIMEAN KHANATE

C R I M E A N   K H A N A T E

L I T H U A N I A

Kiev

Vorskla
1399

Blue Waters
1363

Perekop

Solkhat

Bakhchysaray

Caffa

SEA OF AZOV

B L A C K   S E A

Volga

Ural

Samara

Usha

Volga

Kliazma

Oka

Khoper

Don

Vorskla

Dnieper

Pripet

Dniester

Southern Bug

Danube

Molch

Kuban

Kuma

Scale 1 : 12 500 000

0   100 miles

0   100 kilometers

Copyright © by Paul Robert Magocsi

36

Khan Haji Giray
(d.1466).

While Crimea was still part of the Golden Horde, it served as a refuge for those leaders who failed in their attempts to become khan. Beginning already in the late fourteenth century, some governors in the Golden Horde's administrative center of Solkhat (in particular one Taş Timur) tried to establish an independent political entity based in Crimea. Another unsuccessful contender for the throne of the Golden Horde was Haji Giray, who in 1428 sought refuge in Lithuania, where he remained until invited by local Tatar clans to rule over Crimea.

Haji Giray eventually accepted the invitation, arrived sometime in the late 1430s, and proclaimed the independence of Crimea from the Golden Horde. Af-ter a complicated struggle against various competing political forces in the peninsula, he managed to become the first khan of the Crimean Khanate, ruling from ca. 1441 to 1466, and thereby establishing the state's founding and, in the end, only dynasty—the Girays. Crimea's clan leaders specifically chose Haji Giray because he was a Chinggisid; that is, a direct descendent of Chinggis Khan in the male line. This alleged connection to the Mongol past brought great prestige to the Giray family and contributed to the special place held by their patrimony, the Crimean Khanate, within the larger Ottoman-dominated Turkic world.

In the course of their rise to power, it was inevitable that the first Crimean khans of the Giray family would clash with the rulers of the Golden Horde (who still claimed authority over Crimea), as well as with other forces in the peninsula itself: the Theodoro-Mangup Principality in the peninsula's southwestern mountainous back country; and the Genoese, whose control of trade and the coastal cities posed a particular challenge. In the midst of this three-way struggle for control of Crimea between Girays, the Theodoro princes, and the Genoese, a new contender entered the field—the Ottoman Turks.

For over a century, the Ottoman Turks had systematically conquered various lands of the Byzantine Empire. Finally, Constantinople, the imperial New Rome, fell in 1453. Byzantium was no more. The Ottoman conqueror of the city, Sultan Mehmed II (reigned 1451-1481), was determined to extend his realm north of the Black Sea, and thereby transform it into an "Ottoman lake." In 1475, Ottoman forces arrived in Crimea and captured Caffa, other Black Sea ports, and the mountain-top fortress of Mangup, thereby destroying the Principality of Theodoro. At the same time the sultan rejected the Crimean khan's claim to Caffa and other Black Sea coastal towns, which instead were placed directly under Ottoman administration. Place-name changes symbolized the end of Genoese rule and the ascendancy of Ottomans: Italian Kalamita became Turkish Inkerman, Cembalo—Baliklava (later Balaklava), Soldaia—Sudak, Cerchio—Kerç (today's Kerch), and the main Genoese center, Caffa, became Kefe (today's Feodosiya). Under Ottoman rule, Kefe's port was expanded and its population increased to such a degree that by the early seventeenth century it was one of the largest cities in all of eastern Europe.

The arrival of the Ottomans prompted a new realignment of political power in Crimea. Backed by overwhelming military force, the sultan was able to dictate terms to the Giray rulers of the Crimean Khanate. In return for pledging vassalage to the Ottoman sultan, Crimea's khan at the time, Mengli I Giray (reigned 1478-1515), was able to regain his throne and, with Ottoman military support, gradually impose his authority vis-à-vis rivals within the region. In the end, the Crimean peninsula itself was divided between two political spheres. A narrow strip of non-contiguous territory along the Black Sea littoral became part of an Ottoman province (*sanjak*) named Kefe, after its administrative center. The rest of the peninsula was under the authority of the Crimean khan and clan leaders loyal to him.

From the very beginning the Ottomans maintained a special relationship with the Crimean Khanate and its Giray ruling dynasty. This had to do with the Ottoman sultan's claim of authority over all Turkic peoples that inhabited the vast steppe region stretching from Ukraine

Kerch. Turkish fortress at Eni-Kale, built 1703-1710.

Khan Devlet I Giray (d.1577).

far eastward to Central Asia. Since the Girays were considered direct descendants of Chinggis Khan, the Ottomans used their connection with the Crimean Khanate to associate themselves with the universal Mongol heritage and to legitimize their claims over the Central Asiatic Turkic world. Therefore, in contrast to its other vassal states, which were required to pay tribute and supply troops to the sultan, it was the sultan who provided the Crimean khans with an annual pension as well as landholdings in the Ottoman provinces of Rumelia (the Balkan Peninsula) and Anatolia (modern-day Turkey). And whenever the Ottomans needed troops from Crimea, they addressed an "invitation" to the khan—not an order—and accompanied it with campaign expenses. While it is true that Ottoman interference in Crimean poli-

tics was to increase, this did not really occur until the seventeenth century. Until then, the Crimean Khanate was able to maintain a privileged position within the Ottoman Empire and to follow a basically independent foreign policy—a policy, moreover, that was concerned primarily with the heritage of the Golden Horde.

From the outset of the Crimean Khanate's existence, the Girays claimed authority over all the lands that had once been part of the Golden Horde. This was the position of the founder of the ruling dynasty, Haji Giray, as well as that of his son and successor, Mengli I Giray, who not only captured in 1502 the Golden Horde's capital of New Saray on the lower Volga River, but adopted for himself and his Crimean successors the title, "Great Khan of the Golden Horde and the Kipchak Steppe." Mengli and the Crimean khans who followed him also claimed inheritance to the Golden Horde's right to collect tribute from Poland and Muscovy, claims which not surprisingly brought the Crimean Khanate into conflict with its two Christian neighbors to the north.

The height of Crimean political power and influence was reached in the sixteenth century during the reigns of three talented and effective rulers: Sahib I Giray (r. 1532-1551), Devlet I Giray (r. 1551-1577), and Gazi II Giray (r. 1588-1608). During this era of relative stability and prosperity, the khanate's relationship with the Ottoman Empire was regulated, control of the steppelands north of the Black and Azov seas was secured,

SEA OF
AZOV

Kerch Straits

Kerch

Caffa / Kefe

B L A C K   S E A

Solkhat /
Eski Kïrïm

Sudak

Alushta

Karasu-
bazar

Salgir

Akmechet

Alma

Kïrk
Yer

Bakhchysaray

Mangup

Inkerman

Balaklava

Or-
Kapï

Gözleve

Dnieper

① ① ③ ② ② ④ ⑤ ⑥

Clan territories (beylik)

① Shirin ④ Yashlav
② Barin   ⑤ Mangit/Mansur
③ Argïn   ⑥ Kipchak

Crimean Khanate

Theodoro-Mangup Principality, to 1475

Territory under Ottoman rule

Copyright © by Paul Robert Magocsi

Scale 1 : 2 000 000

50 miles

50 kilometers

0

0

40

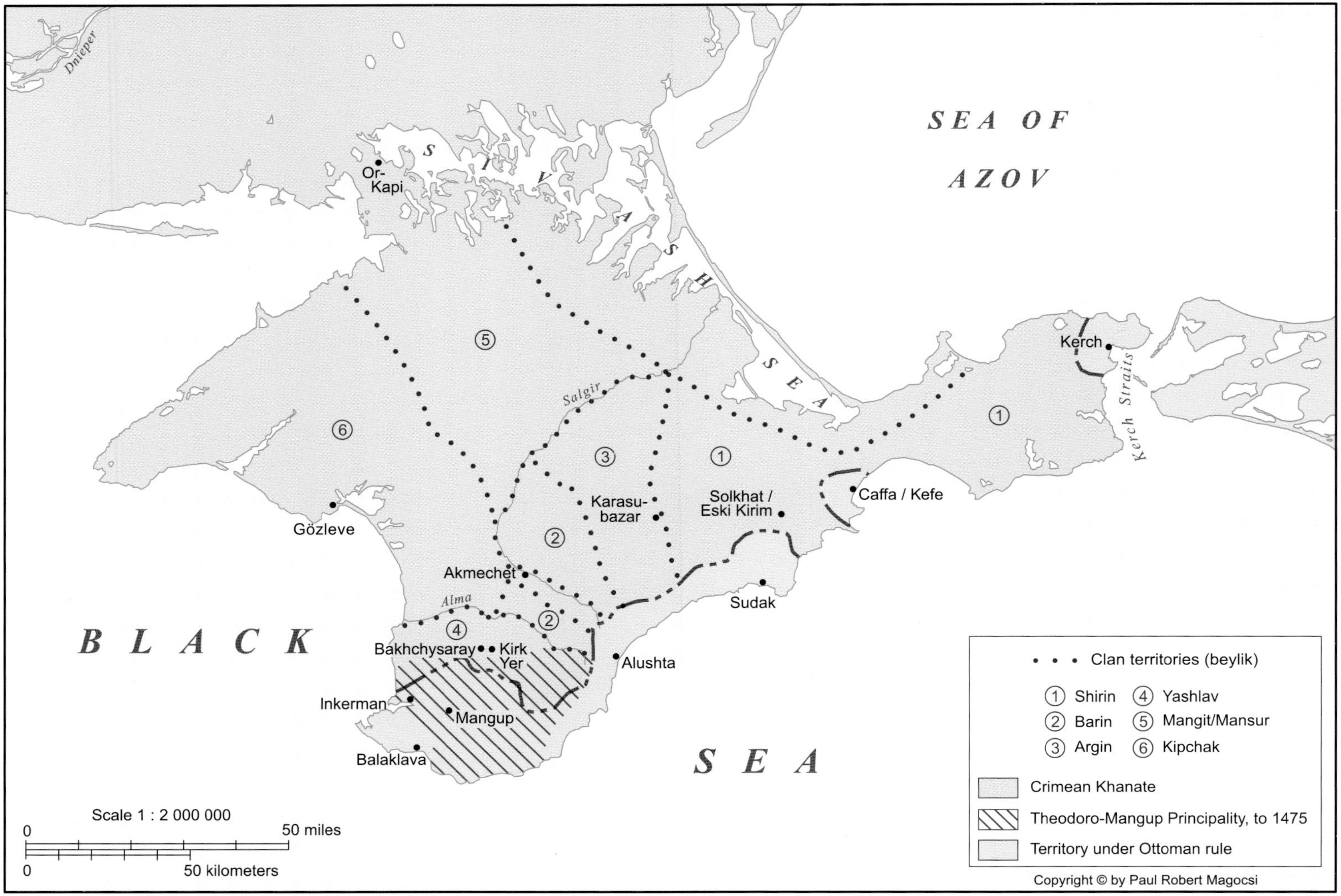

and Bakhchysaray was transformed into a political and cultural center worthy of a state that claimed descent from the Mongol Empire through the Golden Horde.

It was the struggle to regain control of the lands of the Golden Horde and to enforce its tributary rights over countries to the north that brought the Crimean Khanate—sometimes by itself, at other times in cooperation with the Ottoman Empire—into conflict with the other Tatar successor khanates (Astrakhan and Kazan) and especially with the Grand Duchy of Muscovy. Only after Muscovy conquered the Kazan and Astrakhan Khanates in the 1570s did the Girays realize that their dream of replacing the Golden Horde throughout the entire Volga Region had finally ended. From then on they turned their attention elsewhere, in particular to the northwest, as a result of which they were drawn into the expanding Ottoman sphere in the Balkans. This same period, the late sixteenth century, was marked by an ever closer relationship with the Ottoman Empire within which the Crimean Khanate became an increasingly subordinate vassal state.

Whereas the Crimean Khanate's interest in Muscovy was in part political—namely, the restoration of control over lands of the former Golden Horde—their interest in Poland and Lithuania (united into a joint commonwealth in 1569) was driven primarily by economic, not political motives. At times the khanate allied with Poland in campaigns against Muscovy, but more often it saw the Polish-Lithuanian Commonwealth, especially its Ukrainian lands with their Zaporozhian Cossack defenders, as its primary source for slaves. The slave raids did not necessarily preclude alliances between Zaporozhian Cossacks and Crimea's khans whenever their political interests coincided. Those common interests reached a high point during the 1648 Cossack uprising against Poland led by Hetman Bohdan Khmelnytskyi. The Cossack-Crimean alliance, supported by Khan Islam Giray III (r. 1644-1654), was best symbolized by the commander of the Crimean fortress at Perekop, Tughay-Bey. At the head of a 4,000-strong cavalry, he fought alongside Khmelnytskyi, who referred to his deeply trusted ally as "my brother, my soul, the only falcon in the world."[1] Even though the Cossack-Crimean alliance broke down after Khmelnytskyi swore an oath of allegiance to the tsar of Muscovy in 1654, it is useful to note that there was hardly ever the kind of unbridgeable enmity between Slavic Christian Cossacks and Muslim Tatars that subsequent writers would like us to believe.

The Crimean Khanate was a state governed by Islamic law, whose rulers and majority Tatar and Turkic population were Sunni Muslims. The head of state was the khan, always of the Giray dynasty, who derived his preeminent status within the Tatar political leadership because he was a descendant of Chinggis Khan. The Giray khans were not absolute rulers but instead governed with the active participation of Crimean

Tatar clan leaders (*beys*), the most important of which were the so-called *karachi beys*, who initially represented the Barin, Argin, Yashlav, and—most influential of all—the Shirin clan. These four clans as well as the Nogay clans (Mangit/Mansur and Kipchak) derived their social and economic influence from two sources: (1) ownership of large tracts of land, mostly in the steppe zone of the peninsula north of the mountains; and (2) their ability to supply or deny, at their discretion, troops to the khan. The Crimean clan leaders met periodically in assemblies (the *kurultay*), which formally elected a new khan before submitting his candidacy to the Ottoman sultan for approval. Aside from the kurultay, clan leaders, together with clerics and elders of the khan's court, also sat on the khan's council of the state (*divan*), which effectively determined Crimean governmental policy.

Although the Girays remained the ruling dynasty throughout the entire history of the Crimean Khanate, it was not uncommon for there to be competition for access to the throne. In the absence of any fixed order of succession, the throne might be passed on to a close male relative of the ruling khan, possibly one who otherwise functioned as his second (*kal-*

The Ak-Kaya (White Cliff) promontory on the outskirts of Bilohirsk/Karasubazar, legendary site where in 1783 Crimean Tatar aristocracy (beys) pledged their loyalty to the Russian Empire.

gay sultan) or third (*nureddin sultan*) in command. In practice, one or the other rival candidates were supported by Crimea's various clan leaders or by the Ottoman sultan, with the result that succession to the khanate's throne was hardly ever straightforward. Instead, the interregnum after the death of a khan was often marked by conflict and multiple short-lived reigns of khans who, after being deposed, might even return to power after the elimination of their rival.

Like that of most states, the territorial extent of Crimean Khanate changed during its nearly three and one-half centuries of existence from the 1440s to 1783. What remained unchanged, however, was the core of the state, which consisted of the Crimean peninsula itself (except for the Black Sea coastal strip under the Ottomans), as well as lands beyond the Perekop isthmus, specifically the southern Ukrainian steppe between the Sea of Azov and the Dnieper River from its mouth in the west to its first great bend in the east. Aside from this core area, the Crimean Khanate at times included steppelands farther north and east, among which from the mid-sixteenth century was one more or less permanent addition: the historic Kuban region in present-day Russia; that is, the lowland steppe east of the Sea of Azov bounded by the Don, Manich, Egorlik, and Kuban rivers.

Within this vast territory, there were by the mid-sixteenth century an estimated 500,000 inhabitants, broadly divided into two categories: nomadic and sedentary. The nomadic pastoralists lived in the sparsely settled steppe-like plains, which covered the northern two-thirds of the Crimean peninsula as well as southern Ukraine and Kuban. By far the largest number of the khanate's inhabitants were sedentary dwellers living in villages in the foothills and mountain valleys of the peninsula as well as in its coastal towns.

Crimea's peasant farmers were organized in villages; the land was worked in common; and taxes were assigned by the landlord (usually tribal and clan leaders) to the village as a whole. In contrast to Poland-Lithuania and Muscovy, peasants in the Crimean Khanate were never made proprietary serfs and were free to leave the land if they wished. Among the most important and lucrative export products of Crimean agriculture were fruits, tobacco, and honey.

The first capital of the Crimean Khanate was the eastern town of Solkhat/Kirim (today Staryi Krym), but already under Khan Haji Giray in the mid-fifteenth century it was moved closer to the center of the peninsula. He chose the mountain-top town of Kirk Yer, located a few kilometers east of Bakhchysaray. Kirk Yer functioned as a formidable fortress, while in the valley below at Salachik (today Starosillia) the khan had a residential palace. It was Haji Giray's son, Mengli I Giray, who expanded the palace complex at Salachik, which included the Zinjirli *medrese*, or college (est. 1500) to train Muslim clerics. When Salachik proved to be too constrained for the growing Crimean state, one of Mengli's sons, Khan Sahib

TERRITORIAL EVOLUTION OF THE CRIMEAN KHANATE

MAP 7

Scale 1 : 7 000 000

100 miles

100 kilometers

Independent Crimean Khanate, 1774-1783

Boundary of the Russian Empire, 1783

Crimean Khanate

1466   1696

1550   1768

M U S C O V Y

P O L A N D - L I T H U A N I A

N O G A Y

Kiev

Volga

Don

Donets'

Montsh

Don

Tana/Azak

Kuban

Egorlik

C I R C A S S I A N S

S E A   O F   A Z O V

Kerch

Caffa/Kefe

Solkhat

Perekop

Bakhchysaray

Dnieper

Ros

Southern Buh

Dniester

Danube

B L A C K   S E A

I Giray (r. 1532-1550), moved a few kilometers down the valley to Bakhchysaray (Turkic: Bahçesaray), where in 1532 he founded a new palace that was to become the permanent residence of the Crimean khans. With its palace, extensive gardens, mosques, schools, and other public buildings, Bakhchysaray was transformed into an impressive center of Islamic culture as well as the political seat of the Crimean Khanate. It is interesting to note that, while losing its status as the Crimean capital, the mountain-top town of Kirk Yer, later known as Chufut-Kale (which in Crimean Tatar means the Jews' Fortress), retained its importance as the center for the community of Karaites/Karaim, that is Jews who adhere to a form of a non-Talmudic Judaism.

Whereas the Crimean Khanate quickly took on the characteristics of a stable sedentary society associated with the agricultural, artisanal, and commercial pursuits of the majority of the population living in the southern third of the peninsula, there was yet another important element within the khanate's political sphere. These were the Nogay Tatars; that is, Kipchak-speaking nomadic peoples of Turkic origin who pastured their flocks on Ukraine's steppe lands north of the Sea of Azov and the Black Sea stretching from the Kuban River in the east to the Danube River in the west.

The Nogay were originally one of the many tribal groupings within the Golden Horde. In 1556, when Muscovy finally subdued the Astrakhan Khanate and the Nogay heartland east of the Volga River

Starosillya/Salachik, near Bakhchysaray. Mausoleum of the first Crimean khans, built 1501.

and north of the Caspian Sea, a portion of the Nogays migrated westward to the steppe zone in that part of the Crimean Khanate located north of the Sea of Azov and Black Sea. In this region the Nogays themselves were split into several tribal confederations: the Kuban Nogay (east of the Sea of Azov), the Yedichkul Nogay (north of the Sea of Azov), the Jamboyluk Nogay (north of the Crimea), the Yedisan Nogay (between the Southern Buh and Dniester Rivers), and the Bujak Nogay (between the Dniester and Danube Rivers).

These various Nogay tribes, generally referred to in Slavic and Western sources as "Tatars," were nominally under the authority of the Crimean khan, whose authority was expressed in the form of a representative (*serasker*)

sent from Bakhchysaray. In practice, however, the Nogays usually followed their own whims and might even rebel against the khanate's authorities if they felt it was necessary to defend their own interests. "Yet," as the historian Alan Fisher has remarked, "the Nogays served a useful purpose for the Crimean Khanate: They prevented the establishment of solid Slavic settlements in the steppe and provided the Crimean slave markets with a never ending supply of captives."[2] The repeated raids into the heart of Ukraine did, however, provoke a response: the establishment of self-defence groups, which by the second half of the sixteenth century evolved into a worthy opponent for the Nogays and Crimean Khanate—the Zaporozhian Cossacks.

Crimean and Nogay Tatars, *engraving (1844) by unidentified artist.*

46

Slave Market in Smyrna, *engraving (1837)*
by Denis-Auguste Raffet.

By the early sixteenth century, Crimea's economy had come to be based largely on the slave trade. Slavery was legal according to Islamic law, although only persons from outside the Muslim world could be enslaved. Therefore, captives taken in wars against non-Muslim powers were prime candidates for slavery. While slaves formed an integral part of the Ottoman Empire's socioeconomic system, that society allowed for various forms of manumission, both for slaves and their offspring, leading in part to a situation in which the empire was in constant need of replenishing this human commodity. Before long the Ottoman's vassal state, the Crimean Khanate, became its primary source of slaves. From the standpoint of the Crimean authorities, whenever there was a downturn in agricultural productivity the state could supplement its income with profits earned from selling slaves. Just to the north of the Nogay steppe were the non-Muslim lands of Ukraine and southern Russia, which at the time were nominally under the control of Poland, Lithuania, and Muscovy. It was there that Tatars from Crimea turned in search of Christian Slavs to enslave.

The Tatars, whether the khan's calvary or Nogay slave-raiders, followed several invasion routes that began at Perekop. Perekop was also the site of a major defensive fortress (in Tatar: Or-Kapi, "Ditch at the Gate") located at the northern end of the isthmus where the Crimean peninsula joins the mainland Ukrainian steppe. The khanate's military forces, which were almost exclusively cavalry, ranged in size from 10,000 to 30,000 soldiers in the sixteenth century. While the Nogay slave-raiding parties were much smaller, their incursions were more frequent, with the

Was Crimean and Ottoman slavery all that bad?

What happened to captives from Ukrainian lands in Poland-Lithuania and Muscovy when they were brought to Crimea and the Ottoman Empire? For generations accounts from those Christian lands, as well as Ukrainian oral literature (dumy), have included tales of how slaves suffered at the hands of their Crimean and Ottoman masters. And it is true that life was extremely harsh (and often short) for galley slaves conscripted into the imperial naval fleet, or for the smaller numbers for field hands who labored on Ottoman landed estates. Workers in silk manufacturing plants (concentrated in the Anatolian town of Bursa) and house servants fared somewhat better.

There was yet another segment of captives, both male and female, who clearly improved their social and economic status while living in the Ottoman world. These people included converts to Islam, who served in various positions in the Ottoman military administrative system. Females, meanwhile, were often brought into the harems of the Ottoman elite. The most renowned of these was a captive from Galicia, Nastya Lisovska. Known as Roxelana, or Hürrem Sultan (her Ottoman name), she became the favorite wife of Sultan Süleyman I ("the Magnificent") and a personage of political influence in her own right during the apogee of Ottoman power in the mid-sixteenth century. Her privileged status in Ottoman society, remembered by millions of Muslim pilgrims who pray at her mausoleum immediately adjacent to the famed Mosque of Suleiman the Magnificent in the heart of Istanbul, not only is a testament to her own native intelligence and political acumen, but reminds us that perhaps Crimean and Ottoman slavery was not necessarily all that bad.

Portrait of Roxolana
(Hasseki Hürem Sultan)
by an unknown
16th-century painter.

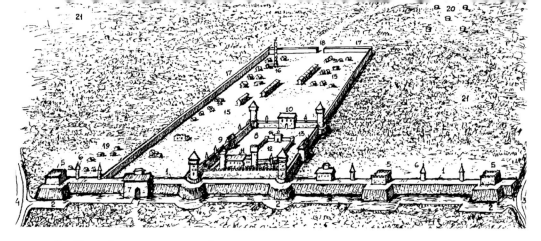

Or-Kapi Fortress at Perekop, 17th century, reconstruction by N. Vitzen.

result that the number of captives they managed to acquire was quite astonishing. Some scholars have estimated an average of 20,000 captives from Poland-Lithuania each year, with total losses from the period 1500-1664 alone reaching about one million people.[3] A certain number of captives were allotted to the Crimean khan and the remainder to all those who participated in a given campaign. Most, however, went to the Ottoman Empire: perhaps a fifth to the sultan as tribute, and the rest sold to Ottoman buyers at the Crimean Tatar slave markets in Bakhchysaray, Karasubazar (today's Bilohirsk), the port of Gözleve (today's Yevpatoriya), but most importantly at the Ottoman-ruled port of Kefe.

The increasing dependence on slavery as the basis of the Crimean economy, let alone the very existence of the khanate as a political entity, was to be directly affected by developments along the khanate's northern frontier. By the end of the seventeenth century, the balance of power in eastern Europe had changed: Poland-Lithuania was on the decline, and Muscovy was quickly replacing it as the dominant force in the region. Muscovy's

long-term goal was to advance farther southward in order to acquire permanent warm-water ports along the Black Sea. To achieve this, Muscovy first had to deal with the Ottoman Empire, which had already reached the height of its power. By the second half of the seventeenth century, Ottoman borders reached their greatest extent and included territory in central Ukraine beyond the Ros River almost as far north as Kyiv. Consequently, the Crimean Khanate found itself caught between what turned out to be a monumental struggle between Muscovy (which in 1721 became the Russian Empire) and the Ottoman Empire.

Even before Russia gained the upper hand in eastern Europe, the status of the Crimean Khanate had changed. By the beginning of the seventeenth century, the Ottomans were playing an increasingly influential role in Crimean politics, including the selection or deposition of the state's ruling khans. No longer was the khanate able to refuse what now became Ottoman orders to supply the sultan with military forces. Even more problematic, however, was the return, or lack of it, that the Crimean

Khanate got from its increasing outlay of troops. As the fortunes of the Ottoman Empire itself declined, so too did income for Crimea's khan and clan leaders in the form of war booty, which at best declined or dried up entirely. By 1700, Muscovy finally stopped its annual tribute payments to the khans, and subsequent Muscovite/Russian military victories and international treaties put an effective end to the export of captives from its lands. All these factors undermined the slave trade which had been the mainstay of Crimea's economy.

By the 1730s, the balance of military power had permanently shifted. Russian armies were able to invade at will Crimean territory, even capturing the capital of Bakhchysaray and destroying the khan's palace in 1736. But it was the Russian-Ottoman war of 1768-1774 that really changed everything. Early in the conflict the Russians managed to gain the allegiance of the Nogay Tatars, which meant the effective loss to the khanate of lands beyond the Crimean peninsula. In late 1770, the khan himself and the Crimea's most powerful clan, the Shirin, decided to abandon their association with the Ottomans and instead to pledge their loyalty to the sovereign of Russia, Empress Catherine II.

It took another year, during which the Ottomans tried to reassert their authority and the Russians sent an army to invade Crimea, before the political situation was clarified. Faced with the reality of tsarist Russian troops in all the key cities of Crimea, representatives of the khanate headed by the heir apparent (*kalgay*) to the throne, Shahin Giray, travelled to the Russian capital of St. Petersburg in November 1771 to negotiate an agreement for an independent state. It was during these negotiations that Empress Catherine was smitten, some say infatuated, by the intelligence, good looks, and European manners of Shahin Giray. Such human interest no doubt helped the Crimean cause. Within a few months, a treaty was signed in the town of Karasubazar (1772) that formally created an independent Crimean state. Crimea was still headed by the Giray dynasty, but it was now under the protection of the Russian Empire. The Ottomans finally accepted the loss of the Crimean Khanate (including their own Kefe province along the peninsula's Black Sea littoral) as part of the provisions of the Treaty of Kuchuk-Kaynardzha (1774) that brought the Russian-Ottoman war to an end.

The first years of independent Crimea were characterized by an internal struggle between Tatar supporters of Russia and those who hoped for the return of Ottoman suzerainty. Tsarist military intervention directed by Catherine's trusted advisor Prince Grigoriy Potemkin ended those controversies, however, and allowed in 1776 for the installation as khan of the pro-Russian Shahin Giray. The new khan set out to transform completely Crimean society through a program of secularization that included an end to Islamic religious law (the Sharia) and equality of all religions. Particular emphasis was given to modernizing the army (trained by Prussians and British) and to the symbolic transfer of the khanate's capital from in-

Empress Catherine II, greeted at Balaklava during her triumphant visit (1787) by 100 "Amazons"— a special company comprised of the wives and daughters of the Russian army's Greek Batalion stationed in Crimea.

land Bakhchysaray to the outward-looking seaport of Kefe/Feodosiia.

Shahin Giray's reforms, both realized and planned, alienated most traditionally-minded clan and Muslim religious leaders who were reluctant to give up their dominant role in Crimea's political and socio-economic life. The increasing social instability contributed to friction between Muslims and Christians, especially in the coastal cities, and to the forced removal at Russia's insistence in 1778 of over 31,000 Christians, mostly Greeks and Armenians. Crimea's Christians were resettled by the Russian imperial government on territory that formerly belonged to the Crimean Khanate: Greeks in and near the newly founded city of Mariupol on the northern shores of the sea of Azov; Armenians farther east near the mouth of the Don River.

It turned out that Khan Shahin was unable to contain the revolts against his regime and restore social stability. The Russian government got tired of support-

ing an unpopular ruler. Consequently, Empress Catherine II heeded Potemkin's suggestion and issued a manifesto in 1783, which unilaterally put an end to the short-lived independent Crimean state and annexed it to the Russian Empire. What remained of the khanate's territory in the peninsula and north of the Sea of Azov was made part of a Russian administrative entity (*guberniya*) called Taurida.

Since the transformation of the Crimean Khanate from an Ottoman to a Russian territory took place during the reign of Empress Catherine II, she was credited with the annexation of 1783. This act made an enormously positive impression on the Russian public and the empire's allies abroad. After all, it was Catherine II who finally fulfilled the age-old dream of the Muscovite and Russian rulers, and it was she who achieved something which none of her predecessors was able to realize: the acquisition of the Crimean peninsula and most of the coastal region north of the Black Sea and Sea of Azov.

Who are the Crimean Tatars?

It is frequently assumed that the Tatars came to Crimea in the mid-thirteenth century as part of the Mongol armies that conquered much of Eurasia. We also know that already during the Mongol invasion the term **Tatar** was a loose term that could not be used to refer to any one people or political entity. The origins of the people known today as Crimean Tatars are much more complex than the simplistic notion of association with the Mongols and the eventual formation of the Crimean Khanate. Instead, the Crimean Tatars evolved from an amalgam of ethnic groups, many of whom have lived in Crimea since time immemorial.

The governing elite of the Crimean Khanate included the extended Giray ruling family and the various clan leaders who administered large tracts of land in the peninsula's steppelands and mountainous regions. Members of this elite were descendents of the Turkic Kipchak nomads and warriors who lived in what became the heartland of the Mongolo-Tatar Golden Horde. Nogay tribes from the same region came in the late sixteenth century and settled in the steppe regions of Crimea where they were henceforth known as Steppe Tatars. The Crimean elite spoke and developed for administrative purposes a written language that was a mixture of Kipchak Turkic (from the Inner Asian steppe) and Oghuz Turkic (related to the Turkish language of Anatolia in the heart of the Ottoman Empire).

In contrast to the khanate's ruling elite, the vast majority of the peninsula's Tatar inhabitants consisted of the descendents of the numerous peoples—whether nomadic pastoralists, sedentary agriculturists, or town dwellers—who for centuries had lived in Crimea: Taurians, Greeks, Scythians, Alans, Goths, Huns, Genoese, Armenians, Jews, Kipchaks, Anatolian Turks, and Slavs. In the course of the fifteenth and sixteenth centuries, these peoples, if they did not already speak some Turkic language, became linguistically turkicized; many also adopted the Islamic religion. The heterogeneous ethnic mix of Turkic-speaking Muslims came to be known as Tats (not to be confused with a numerically small Iranian-speaking people in the Caucasus region). The very term **Tat** reflects their diverse origin. Initially, it was a derogatory word used by Turkic peoples to describe their neighbors (and converts to Islam), who may have spoken some form of Turkic but were not considered of "pure" Turkic descent.

The Tats were not only the peasant farmers of Crimea's mountainous foothills and valleys (who spoke a mixed Kipchak-Oghuz Turkic language), they also made up the majority of coastal town dwellers, the so-called Yaliboyu Tats, who lived under direct Ottoman administration (and who spoke Oghuz Turkic as in Anatolia). The Tats gradually became the dominant demographic element in the peninsula, and together with the Nogay Steppe Tatars they evolved into the Crimean Tatar ethnos with characteristics distinct from the Kazan Tatars in the Volga region and other Turkic-speaking Tatars in the Russian imperial world. In other words, that ethnos was formed from the Tats—whether peasants, artisans, tradespeople, or bureaucrats—and the Nogay/Kipchak tribal clans of Crimea's steppe regions.

The assimilation of Crimea's diverse peoples into the peninsula's Turkic-speaking Islamic majority left a distinct cultural and linguistic imprint on the Tats, who eventually formed the basis of a Crimean Tatar ethnos. For example, the Turkic language of the coastal (Yaliboyu) Tats contains several loanwords from Italian and Greek, reflecting the historic presence of those peoples in Crimea's port cities. There were also a few peoples who, while adopting Turkic speech, did not become Muslims. These included the Christian Armenians and Greeks (the urum, or Greek Tatars) and the Jewish Krymchaks and Karaites. The Armenians and Greeks were concentrated in Kefe (today's Feodosiya). The Krymchaks and Karaites lived primarily in the khanate's largest towns: Akmesjit (today within Simferopol), the port of Gözleve (today Yevpatoriya), the Shirin clan "capital" of Karasubazar (today Bilohirsk), and the khanate's capital Bahçesaray (Bakhchysaray).

Bakhchysaray, lithograph (1842) of the Crimean khan's palace by Carlo Bossoli.

Chapter 5

Crimea in the Russian Empire

With the annexation of Crimea to the Russian Empire in 1783, Empress Catherine II set out to integrate this new territorial acquisition into the rest of the realm. Two decades later, the Crimean peninsula, together with a portion of the Nogay steppe in southern Ukraine between the Dnieper River and the Perekop isthmus, was reorganized into an imperial province called Taurida (Russian: Tavrida), recalling the ancient Greek name for Crimea and its "original" inhabitants. The khan, the extended Giray family, and the khanate's leading administrators, all of whom went into exile, were replaced by a civil administration headed by a governor (Russian: *gubernator*) appointed by, and directly responsible to, the tsar in St. Petersburg. Since Bakhchysaray was the symbol of the conquered khanate, the administrative center of imperial Russian Taurida and the seat of its governor had to be placed elsewhere. The place chosen was the old Tatar town of Akmesjit (Tatar: Aq-Mescit), which was renamed Simferopol.

The initial tone of Russian rule was set by two imperial decrees. Already in 1773, Catherine II had issued an edict of religious toleration, which singled out the Muslim faith and protected it from any interference on the part of the empire's dominant Orthodox Christian Church. Then, in 1785, she issued the Charter of Nobility, which reconfirmed all previous rights of the nobility (Russian: *dvorianstvo*), including exemption from state services and taxes and recognition of all land already held by nobles as their legal property. Catherine hoped that decrees such as these, which applied to the empire as a whole, would make it possible for the Russian administrators to reach an accommodation with the leading elements in traditional Crimean Tatar society, the nobility and clergy.

To be sure, those elements in Crimean Tatar society who feared the onset of tsarist rule and who desired to live in an Islamic state emigrated to the Ottoman Empire. Reasonable estimates place the number of refugees at 20,000 to 30,000. Most were persons closely tied to the last khan, Shahin Giray, as well as Nogay

◀ *Entrance to the Orthodox Dormitian Monastery near Bakhchysaray first built in medieval times, restored in the 1850s and 1990s.*

Coat of arms of the Russian imperial province of Taurida.

Tatars from the southern Ukrainian steppelands in Taurida province.[1]

Despite this initial wave of emigration, Catherine's policies of toleration and accommodation proved successful. After all, for Catherine, Crimea was "the pearl in the tsarist crown," so that in the 1783 decree of annexation she pledged not only herself but her successors "to preserve and defend . . . the property, temples, and ancestral [Muslim] faith of Crimea's inhabitants."[2]

The two most important social elements in Crimean society were the Islamic clergy and Tatar nobility. Both were coopted into the Russian imperial system. Muslim mullahs (heads of community mosques) were given the rank of clerics and made part of a social estate (Russian: *soslovie*) that became hereditary. Being the offspring of a mullah, not religious education or knowledge, was the only criterion for membership in this privileged stratum of the Russian imperial social order. The tsarist government also created as early as 1794 a Spiritual Board to govern all Muslim religious affairs in Taurida province. It was headed by the highest ranking Muslim cleric, the *mufti*, who was appointed by the tsar, given the rank of nobility, and, with other members of the board, assigned a generous salary. In effect, all these Muslim clerics became officials beholden to, and wedded to defending the interest of, the tsarist state. And they, indeed, responded with loyalty to the Russian imperial order of which they were an integral part. As for the larger number of mullahs, as well as the mosques and schools, they were supported by income from the so-called *vakif*; that is, lands held by Muslim institutions that were exempt from state dues and taxes.

Similarly, the khanate's hereditary clan leaders (*beys*) and the more numerous service nobility (*mirza*) were coopted into the imperial system. They were all granted, in accordance with Catherine's 1785 Charter, the status of imperial Russian nobility. Not only were they allowed to keep their existing land holdings (and rights to dues from their peasant inhabitants), Tatar nobles were allotted new lands confiscated from the khan's estates. The Crimean Tatar nobility adapted quickly to the lifestyle and social outlook of their Russian counterparts, with some even adding Russian-sounding suffixes to their surnames (Karashayskiy, Kipchakskiy, Bulgakov).

As for the Crimean Tatar peasants, they were never transformed into proprietary serfs, despite the demands of newly arrived Russian nobles, but they were expected to pay landlords rent in the form of a portion of their harvest. While legally free persons, most peasants became "economically enserfed," in many cases having to submit half of their harvest to the landlord on whose property they lived. By the end of the nineteenth century, the majority of Crimea's peasantry, especially in the steppe region, had become landless and impoverished. One burden, however, was not placed on the shoulders of Crimean Tatar peasants. From the outset of Russian imperial rule, they were exempt from compulsory military service.

After the death of Empress Catherine II in 1796, her generally enlightened policies and sympathetic attitude toward

Crimean Tatars and a Mullah, *lithograph (1862) by Théodore de Pauly.*

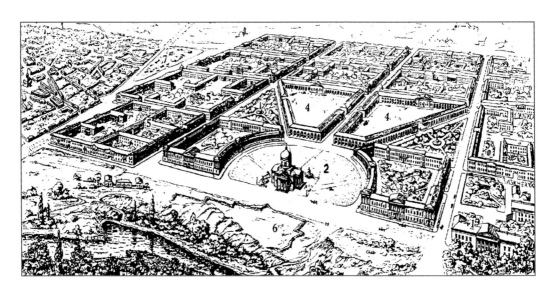

Russian imperial project (1786) for the new city of Simferopol, reconstruction by B. V. Kondratskyi and Yukhym Krykun. 1: stone palace; 2: cathedral church and central square; 3: courtyards of administrative buildings and public schools; 4: market place and stalls; 5: residential sectors; 6: entrenchments; 7: hay market; 8: mediaeval Tatar settlement of Akmesjit.

Crimean Tatar culture continued to be supported by certain imperial officials. Among the most influential was Prince Mikhail Vorontsov, who between 1828 and 1854 served as the governor-general responsible for several provinces in southern Ukraine, including Taurida (of which Crimea was a part). On the other hand, during this same period Tatar cultural monuments, including palaces, parks, fountains, mosques, and cemeteries from the days of the Crimean Khanate were left to decay for lack of up-keep or, in some cases, deliberately destroyed to make way for projects needed by the urban-based Russian imperial administration.

It was also at this time that the peninsula experienced a major demographic change. Large numbers of Tatars left the coastal cities, either moving inland or leaving Crimea permanently by emigrating to the Ottoman Empire. Only inland Bakhchysarai and Karasubazar were officially declared Tatar enclaves. As a result of these departures, certain cities like Kefe (renamed Feodosiya) and Gözleve (renamed Yevpatoriya), lost their importance, while at the same time the Russian imperial administration encouraged the development of new cities, in particular the governmental center at Simferopol (formerly Tatar Aq-Mescit) and, most especially, the new port at Sevastopol (near ancient Chersonesus and more recently the site of the small Tatar village of Agyar). Sevastopol was most importantly home to the Black Sea Fleet, the brainchild of Prince Potemkin created in the 1780s. The fleet quickly became the pride of the tsarist military and the primary bastion for projecting imperial Russia's naval power into the Black Sea and eventually the Mediterranean.

The Russian imperial authorities encouraged settlers from abroad—Germans, Bulgarians, Armenians, Greeks, among others—to settle in Crimea. They were initially less successful, however, in attracting Russians and other East Slavs from within the empire, whose numbers (about 11,000 in the 1790s) remained small until the first half of the nineteenth century.

The government had no trouble, however, attracting nobles of diverse ethnic origin from various parts of the Russian Empire as well as some foreign businessmen to make Crimea their new source of livelihood, wealth, and pleasure. At the very outset of Russian imperial rule in the 1780s and 1790s, the government parcelled out huge swaths of land (confiscated from the exiled khans and Ottoman officials) in the form of outright grants to Russian nobles, the lion's share going to Prince Grigoriy Potemkin. In subsequent decades, further land grants were bestowed on nobles as recognition for some service to the state, or in the form of leases to foreign businessmen. It is in this way that the hero of the Napoleonic Wars, Count Mikhail Vorontsov, and noble families like the Potockis, Naryshkins, and others acquired landed estates in Crimea. Count

▲ *Tatar Homestead in Alupka,*
lithograph (mid-19th century)
by Carlo Bossoli.

Prince Grigoriy Potemkin
(1739-1791),
painting (ca. 1790)
by Johann Baptist von Lampi.

CRIMEA IN THE 19th CENTURY RUSSIAN EMPIRE

MAP 8

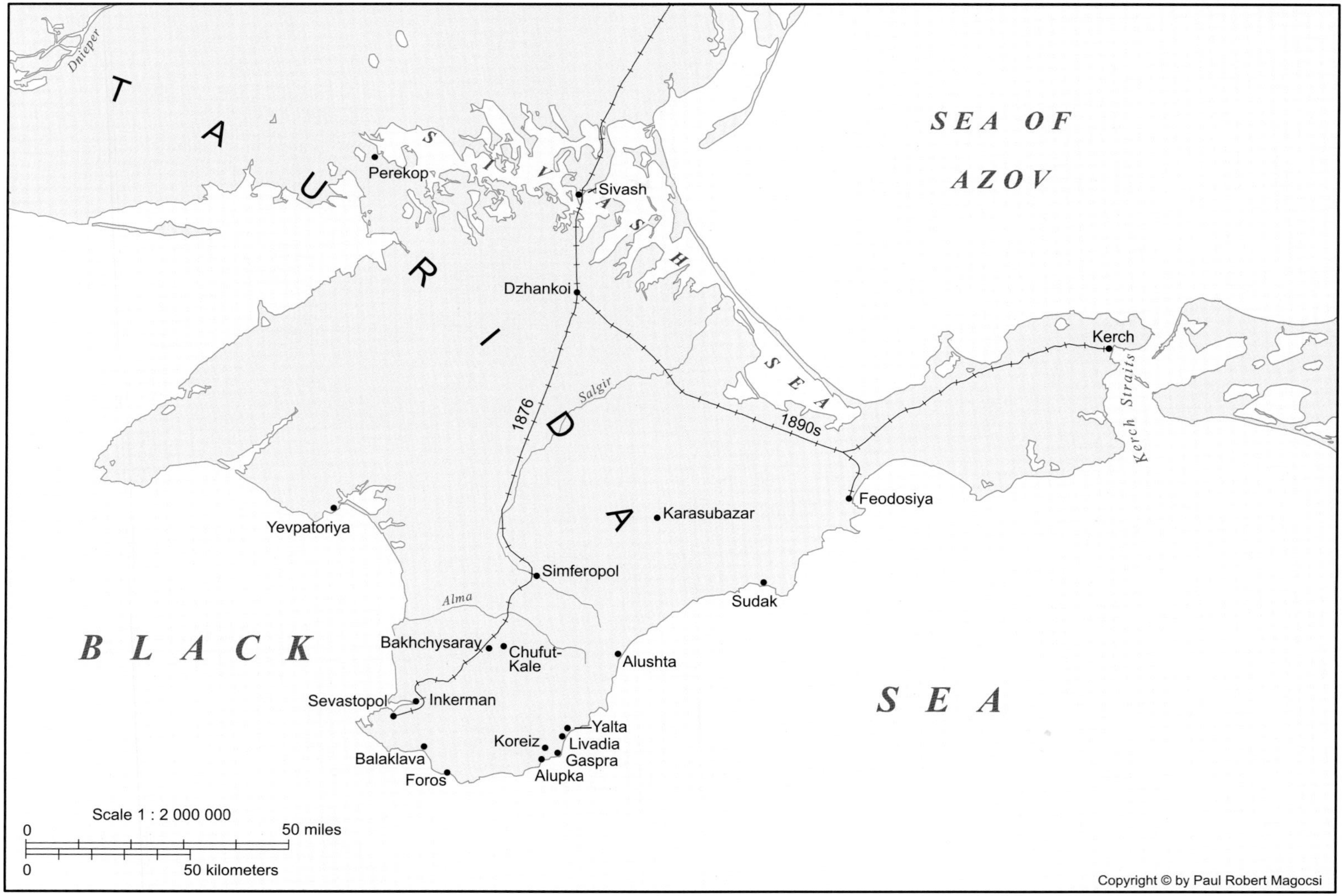
Dnieper
T A U R I D A
SEA OF AZOV
SIVASH SEA
Perekop
Sivash
Dzhankoi
Kerch
Kerch Straits
Salgir
1876
1890s
Feodosiya
Karasubazar
Yevpatoriya
Simferopol
Alma
Sudak
BLACK SEA
Bakhchysaray
Chufut-Kale
Alushta
Sevastopol
Inkerman
Yalta
Koreiz
Livadia
Gaspra
Balaklava
Alupka
Foros
Scale 1 : 2 000 000
0
50 miles
0
50 kilometers
Copyright © by Paul Robert Magocsi

Vorontsov, for instance, developed the famous Massandra winery near Yalta, while a foreign lessee from France, Joseph Blanc, did the same for vineyards in the Sunny Valley just east of Sudak.

Aristocratic families from the north, attracted by Crimea's mild climate and inspired by its exotic cultural and physical landscape, were determined to make their stay—whether for the season or all year long—as elegant and comfortable as possible. Hence arose the handsome residence (1826-1827) of Prince Naryshkin in Simferopol and the truly stunning palaces and European-style gardens and parks, among which were the Potocki manor house (1834) at Livadia near Yalta, the Vorontsov palace (1833-1848) at Alupka, and the Golitsyn palace (1836) at Gaspra.

Count Mikhail Vorontsov (1782-1856), painting (1812) by Alessandro Molinari.

Simferopol. Salgirka Residence of Prince Naryshkin and later Prince Vorontsov, possibly designed by Philip Elson, built 1826-1831.

▲ *Alupka. Vorontsov Palace below Mount Ai-Petri, built 1833-1848 according to designs by Edward Blore as it originally appeared before removal of the Indian-style roof pavilions.*

▶ *Neo-Tudor Gothic-style dining hall (1840s) in the Vorontsov Palace at Alupka.*

Beginning in the 1820s, the imperial government was more successful in encouraging the settlement of Russians from the north, who accounted for more than 70,000 of Crimea's inhabitants at mid-century. As the overall population of the peninsula grew—from 185,000 in 1780s to 250,000 in the 1850s—there was at the same time a proportional decrease in the peninsula's Tatar inhabitants from ninety to sixty percent.[3] The absolute number of Crimean Tatars was to decline even further during the second half of the nineteenth century, a phenomenon that was related to a new war and its aftermath.

In 1854, Crimea was suddenly thrust into the imagination of modern-day Europeans. This was a result of a growing conflict of interest among the continent's so-called Great Powers—Britain, France, Prussia, and Austria—who were increasingly concerned with Russia's growing influence in the Ottoman Empire and its desire since the days of Catherine II to gain control of the Bosporus, Constantinople, and free access to the Mediterranean. Anxious to protect their own commercial interests in the region, Britain and France felt obliged to come to the defence of the Ottoman Empire. In response to a Russian military incursion into the Ottoman-ruled Balkans, a joint British and French fleet crossed the Black Sea and in September 1854 disembarked along the coast of the western Crimea. Their object was to move south and capture the port and Russia's Black Sea Fleet at Sevastopol. The Crimean War had begun, and at the cost of tens of thousands of soldiers who died from combat wounds and disease, the invaders laid siege to the strategic fortresses (Inkerman and Balaklava) surrounding Sevastopol. After a heroic defence by Russian forces, the largely destroyed city finally fell in September 1855. Russia had lost the war.

The bloody conflict undermined Crimea's economy and, in general, revealed the internal weakness of tsarist rule and the need for reform in the empire as a whole. The war also left an undeniable imprint both on the victo-

Sinking Ships of the Russian Black Sea Fleet During the Raid against Sevastopol, 11 September 1854, *painting (1906) by Ivan Vladimirov.*

Russian defense battery at Sevastopol during the Crimean War. Photograph (1855) by James Robertson.

rious British and French, as well as on the defeated subjects of the Russian tsar, whose belletrists, publicists, historians, architects, sculptors, and painters subsequently created a wide range of literary images, buildings, and statues commemorating the events of the Crimean War—images that were to remain imbedded in the historical consciousness of millions of citizens of those countries for generations to come.

While it is true that some Crimean Tatars, unhappy with Russian rule, lent their support to the invading forces, especially at Yevpatoriya, Perekop, and Feodosiya, most remained loyal tsarist subjects. Volunteer Tatar regiments within the Russian ranks were reputed to have fought with distinction against the French and British. Nevertheless, some tsarist officials and, in particular, Russian Orthodox clerics led by Archbish-

op Innokentiy (Borisov), associated all Crimean Tatars with collaboration. The anti-Tatar mood of the post-Crimean War years also encouraged noble landlords to exploit further the peasantry. All these factors produced what certain ruling circles really wanted: the removal of "alien" Muslims from Crimea. The result was the largest of all emigrations. By 1863, official Russian statistics reported the permanent departure of over 140,000 Crimean Tatars to the Ottoman Empire, with the result that 784 villages and hamlets were left abandoned.[4] And all this was happening during the reign of Alexander II, the initiator of the Great Reforms and emancipation of serfs. The "tsar-liberator" for most subjects of the Russian Empire became for Crimean Tatars the "tsar-oppressor."

As Muslims, the Crimean Tatar emigrants sought refuge in the relatively

64

nearby sacred "land of the Caliph"; that is, in the Ottoman Empire, whether in Anatolia, the capital Constantinople, or in peripheral regions in the Balkans. Since, however, the Ottoman Empire itself was in the course of the nineteenth century being steadily reduced in size, certain communities in the Crimean diaspora were before long to find themselves in new countries. Hence, Crimean Tatars who had earlier gone to Circassia north of the Caucasus or to the Bujak (between the lower Dniester and Danube Rivers), eventually found themselves in the Russian Empire, while those settled in the Black Sea coastal region of Dobruja were by the late 1870s living in Romania and Bulgaria. Such

border changes prompted a second emigration from Dobruja in 1877-1878, when between 80,000 to 90,000 Crimean Tatars moved to the Ottoman heartland of Anatolia.[5] It was these various nineteenth-century waves of emigrants who formed the heart of the Crimean Tatar and Nogay diasporan communities that still exist in Romania, Bulgaria, and most especially Turkey and that at various times have continued to maintain ties with their ancestral homeland.

The Russian imperial government made up for these population losses by providing special privileges (financial and social) to settlers from other parts of the empire willing to settle in Crimea. And the newcomers came—Greeks,

Officers of the Crimean Tatar imperial household guard in uniforms from the period 1850-1864.

65

Bulgarians, Armenians, Germans, and Jews, but most especially Russians and Ukrainians—increasing the population of Crimea to 546,000 in 1897. As for the Crimean Tatars, they were reduced to a mere 35 percent of the inhabitants.[6]

The second half of the nineteenth century witnessed the apogee of Russian imperial influence. Crucial to the Russian presence was the ability to reach Crimea from the far north. This was made easier by the completion in 1875 of a railway line that linked St. Petersburg and Moscow to southern Ukraine, and from there via a bridge across the narrow strait near the village of Sivash across Crimea's flat northern plain to the provincial capital of Simferopol and further on to the terminus at the port

The Crimean painter of Azov Greek background, Arkhyp Kuindzhi (1841-1910), portrait (1869) by Viktor Vasnetsov.

German colonists in Crimea, postcard (1860s).

city of Sevastopol. Even earlier, in 1848, a road was built along the coast connecting Sevastopol to Yalta, which thereafter quickly became the center of Crimea's "Riviera." It was Yalta and other nearby coastal towns that were reachable by carriage roads along the coast or by boats along the sea, which became the playground of the Russian imperial elite.

To cater to aristocratic tastes, a whole array of elegant palaces, parks, spas, hotels, and casinos were built in a range of historical architectural styles that were so popular throughout nineteenth-century Europe. The tsars themselves set the tone by constructing summer residences for the royal family just to the east and west of Yalta: the neo-Renaissance palace of Alexander III at Massandra (1892-1902) and the monumental

Sokolyne/Kokközy. Yusupov family palatial hunting lodge, designed by Nikolai Krasnov with Crimean Tatar motifs, built 1908-1910.

neo-Classic palatial complex of Nicholas II at Livadiya (1905-1906). Aristocrats and wealthy business entrepreneurs followed suit and engaged leading architects to build impressive residences, such as the Moresque-style Dulber Palace for the Romanov Prince Petr Nikolaevich at Miskhor (1895-1897), the palace of the Yusupov princes at Koreyiz (1909), and the most romantic of all, the miniature castle known as Lastochkino Gnezdo (Swallow's Nest, 1912) perched on a cliff's edge overlooking the sea near Haspra, for the German entrepreneur, Baron von Steingel.

These and numerous other palaces and villas attracted Europe's and the Russian Empire's leading creative talent,

Massandra. Imperial family palace, designed by Étienne Bouchard and Maximilian Messmacher, built 1881-1882, 1892-1902

whether for artistic inspiration, health reasons, or simply pleasure. Already during the first half of the nineteenth century Crimea had inspired two of the Slavic world's greatest national bards: Poland's Adam Mickiewicz, who was a frequent visitor to Yevpatoriya, and Russia's Aleksander Pushkin, who immortalized for all his readers the "Fountain of Bakhchysaray" as the poetic symbol of unrequited love within the exotic world of the khan's palace. But it was the last four decades of imperial rule before the outbreak of World War I that turned Crimea, especially its Black Sea coast, into an almost required destination for a whole host of creative and performing artists. Among the most renowned to spend extensive periods or repeated visits in Crimea were the Russian writers Leo Tolstoy, Anton Chekhov, and Maxim Gorky; the Ukrainian poetess Lesya Ukraïnka and humorist poet Stepan Ru-

Lesya Ukrayinka (1871-1913), photograph (1897) during one of her extended stays in Crimea.

danskyi; the Belarusan poet Maksym Bohdanovych; the painter of Azov Greek background Arkhip Kuindzhi; the painter and poet-philosopher Maksimilian Voloshyn; the Armenian composer Aleksander Spediarov; and the opera singer Fedor Shaliapin. Among native-born Crimeans whose professional careers were closely linked to their homeland were the archaeologist Aleksandr Berte-Delagard and two natives of Feodosiya: the landscape painter Konstantin Bogaevskiy, and the enormously popular seascape artist of Armenian heritage, Ivan Aivazovskiy.

Maxim Gorky, Feodor Shaliapin, and Stepan Skitalets during a visit (1916) to the costal resort of Foros.

Prince Lev Golitsyn (1845-1915).

As well as being a place of pleasure and creativity, Crimea was the workplace of numerous medical practitioners (Sergei Botkin, Vladimir Dmitriev, and Stepan Rudanskyi, among others), who contributed to the modernization of Crimea's health facilities (especially in the Black Sea coastal towns and cities) and to research in the use of the region's natural resources for medicinal cures. Finally, Crimea became a source of financial profit for savvy businessmen from the imperial north who were able to develop, with the help of local Tatar, Bulgarian, and other farmers, the fruit-growing industries. None were more successful than the few individuals who decided to renew Crimea's wine industry, which dated back to classical times but was left to decline during the period of the Crimean Khanate and Ottoman rule. The renewal of

vineyards and wine production begun in the first half-century of Russian rule by Prince Grigoriy Potemkin and Prince Mikhail Vorontsov was continued in the second half of the nineteenth century by the highly successful Crimean-born merchant of Greek origin, Georgiy Khristoforov, and by Prince Lev Golitsyn, who in the 1890s began marketing the world famous wines produced at the estate of Massandra near Yalta.

While the Russian imperial government and intellectual elite was transforming the secular face of Crimea, the Orthodox Church was very active in trying to deepen the Christian presence in the region. Orthodox prelates began from the proposition that Crimea had originally been a Christian land, and that after several centuries of "foreign"

Archbishop Innokentiy (Borisov, 1800-1857).

69

Islamic predominance it should return to its Byzantine-rite Eastern Orthodox Christian roots. The re-Christianization process took on increasing intensity after the Crimean War and was spearheaded by the archbishop of Taurida, Innokentiy (Borisov).

Beginning in 1850, Archbishop Innokentiy initiated a program to restore "ancient holy places in the Crimean Mountains," with the goal to transform Crimea into "Russia's Athos"—the allusion being to Eastern Orthodoxy's holiest monastic center, Mount Athos, along the coast of northern Greece.[7] The several Crimean sites slated for renewal soon became centers not only for monastic prayer and contemplation, but also pilgrimage destinations for the Orthodox faithful throughout the Russian Empire. These included monasteries at Inkerman, Chersonesus, and Balaklava, the "healing waters" (Savluk-Su) of the Cosmos and Damian spring in the mountains north of Alushta, and, most important of all, the Dormition Monastery near Bakhchysaray.

This last project reflected the particular challenges faced by those—then and still today—concerned with cultural reclamation in multicultural Crimea. Within the space of three kilometres along the gorge east of Bakhchysaray were found holy and commemorative sites of three peoples. At the base of the valley was the tombstone of the first Crimean khan, Haji Giray, and the sixteenth-century Muslim theological academy (Zinjerli *medrese*). Along the cliffs was the Orthodox Dormition Monastery built by Greeks as part of their eighth-century settlement known as Ma'iamdere (from which the city of Mariupol along the Sea of Azov derives its name). In the immediately adjacent upper valley was a Karaite cemetery. And just above it, on the mountain-top Karaite town of Chufut-Kale (itself built on the site of the earlier capital of the Crimean Khanate, Kirk-Yer), was the burial place of Janike, the beloved daughter of the Golden Horde's late fourteenth-century ruler, Tokhtamysh.

Orthodox ideologists had a particular take on the Crimean Tatars within their midst. In effect, they accepted the view that the Crimean Tatars were descendants of an ethnically mixed population, including many European peoples, who had lived on the peninsula from time immemorial. At some point

Chufut-Kale/Kirk Yer. Mausoleum of the Golden Horde princess Janike, built in the early 15th century.

Yalta. Alexander Nevskiy Russian Orthodox Cathedral, designed by Nikolai Krasnov, built 1892.

after the Mongol invasion they were converted from Christianity to Islam. Therefore, the goal of the Orthodox Church was not "to convert" the Tatars, but "to return" them to their alleged ancestral faith. It was with this in mind that Archbishop Innokentiy introduced the Crimean Tatar language as a subject at the Orthodox Seminary in Odessa, the object being to train missionary priests to spread Christianity among the Muslims of Crimea.

Equally important for the Orthodox Christian reclamation project was the construction of a series of monumental churches throughout Crimea: the most prominent were those built in Simferopol (Alexander Nevskiy Cathedral, 1829-1881), Sevastopol (St. Vladimir Equal to the Apostles, 1858-1888),

Yalta (Alexander Nevskiy Cathedral, 1892), Foros (Resurrection, 1892), Feodosiya (St. Catherine's, 1892), Sevastopol (Holy Mother of God the Protectress, 1892-1905), and Yevpatoriya (St. Nicholas the Wonder Worker, 1893-99). The very presence of these imposing architectural structures was intended to remind the inhabitants on a daily basis that Crimea was a Russian and an Orthodox Christian land.

The process of Christianizing Crimea reached its apogee when church historians and archaeologists, excavating at Chersonesus (on the far western edge of modern Sevastopol), were able to demonstrate to their satisfaction that the grounds of the Orthodox monas-

Foros. Russian Orthodox Church of the Resurrected Christ, designed by Nikolai Chagin, built 1888-1892.

*Tsar Nicholas II greeting Russian army officers stationed in Crimea
in the courtyard of the imperial residence at Livadiya
near Yalta (1912).*

tery encompassed the original site of the conversion to Christianity in the 980s of Grand Prince Vladimir/Volodymyr of Kyiv. This meant that Crimea took on a very special place in Orthodox tradition as "the cradle of Russian Christianity." And to drive the point home for future generations, Tsar Alexander II inaugurated the construction at Chersonesus of the monumental St. Vladimir Cathedral (1861-1892).

As Crimea was being refashioned into an imperial "Russian" land, the vast majority of Crimean Tatars were surviving more or less at a subsistence level, either as small-scale artisans in Bakhchysaray, Karasubazar, and a few other towns, or as tenant farmers working on small plots in the mountain valleys beyond the coastal region and on the lowland plains farther north. The Russian imperial regime did make an effort to address the needs of this population, in particular through the *zemstvos*, which were local self-governing agencies formed in the context of the tsarist government's efforts at political and social reform. The work of the *zemstvos* beginning in the late 1870s was particularly important in the areas of education and hygiene. The government also invested large sums of money in elementary schools and medical facilities. Nevertheless, by the end of the century the

Simferopol district, for example, had only one doctor for every 14,000 inhabitants. Even in the highly developed Yalta district along the coast, there was only one doctor for every 7,000 inhabitants. Despite the government's modernization efforts, most Crimean Tatars continued to follow the traditional lifestyle handed down to them by their forbears since the days of the Crimean Khanate and preserved by the conservative policies of the established Muslim clergy. It was in reaction to the stagnation and backwardness of Crimean Tatar society that a few individuals set out to change the status quo in order to improve social conditions among their people.

Throughout the nineteenth century, many peoples of Europe who did not have their own state and who likely lacked cohesion as a distinct community experienced what came to be known as a national awakening. The goal of these national awakenings, or revivals, was to raise the educational, cultural, and socioeconomic status of a given ethnonational group, in order to gain recognition and political rights in the state where it resided. National awakenings were in most cases not the work of the state, but rather of self-appointed patriotic activists, the so-called nationalist intelligentsia, who were convinced that their calling in life was to improve the status of "their" people.

Sometime in the 1880s, Crimea became the birthplace of a national revival on behalf of Tatars and Turkic peoples throughout the Russian Empire. The movement was initiated by Ismail Gas-pirali, also known by the Russian form of his surname, Gasprinskiy. Gaspirali was a teacher in the upper level theological academy (*medrese*) attached to the mosque in his native town of Bakhchysaray. He, therefore, understood very well the negative role played by the clergy-controlled *medrese* and elementary schools (*mektep*), whose primary goal was the inculcation of religious beliefs and, at best, a basic knowledge of the Koran and the tenets of Islam. All subjects were in Arabic, however, a language which the local population did not even remotely understand.

Knowing that such an "education" was incapable of preparing students to

Ismail bey Gaspirali/Gasprinskiy (1851-1914).

Masthead of the Crimean Tatar-Russian newspaper Terjüman/Perevodchik
(The Interpreter).

function in a secular society, Gaspirali proposed what he called the New Method (Usûl-ü Jedid), an educational reform program which called for the introduction of courses in history, geography, and mathematics, which were to be taught using "modern" languages—Russian and Turkish. Such a radical approach to train young people provoked opposition on the part of the established state-supported Muslim school authorities. They were even less enthusiastic about Gaspirali's emancipatory ideas that women should be treated equally with men and that young girls should be required to attend at least elementary school. Finally, Gaspirali also tried to stem the tide of Crimean Tatar emigration to the Ottoman Empire.

The historic Crimean capital of Bakhchysaray was the center of Gaspirali's activity, and it was there that he

Crimean New Method Tatar school.

Staff of the Crimean Tatar newspaper Vatan Hâdimi *(Servant of the Fatherland); editor-in-chief Abdüreshid Mehdi seated second from the right.*

founded the newspaper *Terjüman/Perevodchik* (The Interpreter, 1883-1914), which he hoped would enhance the idea of cultural unity between the Crimean Tatars and other Tatars and Turkic peoples of Muslim faith in the Russian Empire. With this goal in mind, the non-Russian part of his newspaper and other publications were written in Ottoman Turkish, although in a simpler form which omitted florid Arabic and Persian vocabulary and phrases, and replaced them with words from the Crimean Tatar vernacular (spoken language).

Despite Gaspirali's educational and cultural achievements, he was the object of widespread criticism. Conservative Muslim religious leaders (*mullahs*) op-

Title pages (left and right) of the Russian-language journal Narodnaya shkola *(Public School, 1910) published in Bakhchysaray by Ismail Gaspirali, and the Crimean Tatar journal* Âlem-i-Nisvân *(Women's World, 1906-07) edited by his daughter (center), the women's movement leader Shefika Hanim Gaspirali (1886-1975).*

Abdüreshid Mehdi/
Mediev (1880-1912).

Jafar Seydamet
(1889-1970).

Noman Chelebi-Jihan/
Chelebiev (1885-1918).

posed his secular orientation and New Method schools, while supporters of the Crimean Tatar revival challenged his views on national identity. Debates centered on a few key issues. Did the Crimean Tatars form a distinct nationality and, if so, should they have their own literary language? Or, did the adoption of Turkish imply that they were only a branch of a single pan-Turkic entity?

By the beginning of the twentieth century, a new generation of intellectuals known as the Young Tatars (Genç Tatarlar), who were based in Karasubazar (today Bilohirsk) instead of Bakhchysaray, moved beyond Gaspirali's primarily cultural interests to more social and political concerns. They also made Crimea and its Tatars, instead of all Turkic peoples of the Russian Empire, their primary focus, even though the language of their publications, including the newspaper *Vatan Hâdimi* (Servant of Fatherland, 1909-12), favored the idea of Turkish linguistic unity through the medium of Ottoman Turkish. One of the leading Young Tatar activists, Abdüreshid Mehdi, was elected to imperial Russia's parliament, the Second Duma of 1906, on a program committed to the reacquisition of lands lost by Crimean Tatars over the past century. The question of Crimean Tatar particularism versus pan-Turkic unity and the related issues of an appropriate literary language and national identity remained unresolved until the 1920s.

Aside from Gaspirali's supporters and the Young Tatars, there was a third orientation within the Crimean Tatar national revival. This was comprised of students who completed their high school education in Crimea, but who then went to the Ottoman capital of Istanbul to continue their studies at the university level. Istanbul had already in the course of the nineteenth century become a major center of the Crimean Tatar diaspora. There, under the leadership of Noman Chelebi-Jihan (Çelebi Cihan;

Ceremony in Bakhchysaray (1893) for the tenth anniversary of the newspaper
Terdjüman/Perevodchik.

in Russian sources: Chelebiev) and Jafar Seydamet (Cafer Seydamet), the Crimean Student Association (Kirim Talebe Cemiyeti, est. 1908) and its offshoot, the underground Vatan/Fatherland Society (Vatan Cemiyeti, est. 1909), were set up to promote the Crimean Tatar national revival in the homeland. In preparation to achieve that goal, for nearly a decade beginning in 1908, several enthusiasts returned from the Ottoman Empire to Russian-ruled Crimea, bringing with them books and other national literature which they distributed as teachers who worked in Gaspirali's New Method school system. The most famous of this new generation of cultural enlighten-ers was Shevki Bektöre, the renowned patriotic poet born in Romanian-ruled Dobruja, who moved to Turkey until returning to the land of his ancestors in 1909 as an elementary school teacher.

By the outset of the twentieth century, it was clear that the Crimean Tatar national awakening started a few decades earlier by Gaspirali had succeeded in establishing firm roots. The Crimean Tatar awakening, like that of national movements among other stateless peoples in the Russian Empire, was to be profoundly influenced by events unfolding far from their homeland. These events were connected with the outbreak of World War I in August 1914.

Whose heroic Crimea?

The Russian Empire may have lost the Crimean War, but the conflict is celebrated to this day. Most actively remembered is the defense of Sevastopol, commemorated as one of the country's great national epics. The eleventh-month siege in 1854-1855, in which the Russian Army lost 102,000 killed or wounded and hundreds of thousands more from disease, was immortalized in The Tales of Sevastopol. This widely read literary work was written by none other than Russia's greatest nineteenth-century novelist, Leo Tolstoy, who as a young officer fought in the ranks of the besieged at Sevastopol. Since then, millions of ordinary citizens of the Russian Empire and later the Soviet Union have been reminded of the conflict and its heroes—Admirals Pavel Nakhimov, Vladimir Kornilov, and Vladimir Istomin—through a museum of the history of the Black Sea Fleet as well as a panorama (life-size circular painting). The building housing the panorama first opened 1905, and although destroyed during World War II it was carefully restored and re-opened in 1954. The siege of Sevastopol also prompted important medical advances, in particular by the Russian physician and "father of field surgery," Nikolai Pirogov, who invented new life-saving amputation techniques and who was the first doctor to use anesthesia on the battlefield.

For western Europeans and the English-speaking world in general—if they have even heard of Crimea—it is usually because of the war of 1853-1855. French military sacrifices are remembered in the name of a main thoroughfare in Paris, the Boulevard Sebastopol.

Charge of the Light Brigade near Balaklava, 25 October 1854,
lithograph (1885) by William Simpson.

A British nurse tending a wounded soldier in the Crimea War.

Generations of school children in the United Kingdom have all learned about the heroic service rendered by the founder of modern nursing, Florence Nightingale, who, with her staff of 38 female nurses selflessly tended to the sick and wounded within the British ranks. Despite a plaque (now half-hidden by a vineyard and already in a decrepit state) placed in 2004 by the United Kingdom's Prince Philip on the occasion of the one-hundred-fiftieth anniversary of the Battle of Balaklava, it is through literature that the English-speaking world is reminded of the Crimean War. In 1855, the poet laureate of the British Empire, Alfred Lord Tennyson, wrote "The Charge of the Light Brigade," a poem inspired by the heroic but foolishly futile British attack against Russian enemy lines at Balaklava.

> Half a league, half a league
> Half a league onward,
> All in the Valley of Death
> Rode the six hundred
> "Forward, the Light Brigade!
> Charge for the guns," he said:
> Into the Valley of Death
> Rode the six hundred.

And, in words that are understood everywhere by soldiers who are required to follow the orders of their officers, no matter what the cost:

> Theirs not to make reply,
> Theirs not to reason why,
> Theirs but to do or die.

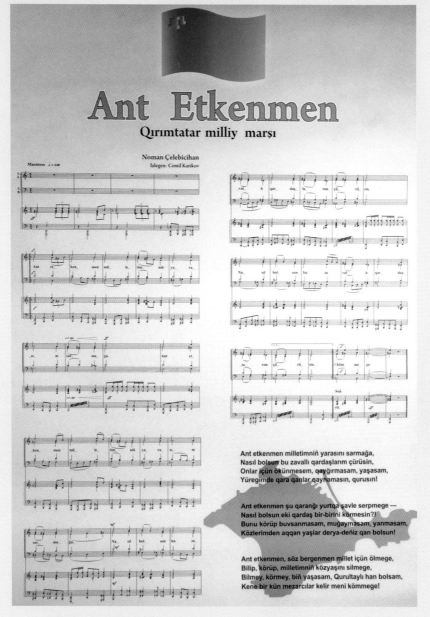

Ant Etkenmen

Qırımtatar milliy marşı

Noman Çelebicihan
İşlegen: Cemil Karikov

Ant etkenmen milletimniñ yarasını sarmağa,
Nasıl bolsun bu zavallı qardaşlarım çürüsin,
Onlar içün ökünmesem, qayğırmasam, yaşasam,
Yüregimde qara qanlar qaynamasın, qurusın!

Ant etkenmen şu qarañğı yurtqa şavle serpmege —
Nasıl bolsun eki qardaş bir-birini körmesin?!
Bunu körüp buvsanmasam, muğaymasam, yanmasam,
Közlerimden aqqan yaşlar derya-deñiz qan bolsun!

Ant etkenmen, söz bergenmen millet içün ölmege,
Bilip, körüp, milletimniñ közyaşını silmege,
Bilmey, körmey, biñ yaşasam, Qurultaylı han bolsam,
Kene bir kün mezarcılar kelir meni kömmege!

I pledge to heal the wounds of Tatars,
Why should my unfortunate brothers rot away;
If I don't sing, don't grieve for them, and if I live,
Let the dark streams of the blood of my heart go dry!

I pledge to bring light to that darkened country,
How may two brothers not see one another?
And when I see this, if I don't get distressed, hurt, seared,
Then let the tears that flow from my eyes become a river, a sea of blood!

I pledge and give my word to die [for my nation],
Knowing, seeing, and trying to wipe away the teardrops of my nation.
Even if I live a thousand unknowing and unseeing years,
Even if I become the Assembly's leader [khan of the Kurultay],
One day the gravediggers will come to bury me!

Chapter 6

Crimea in War and Revolution

The revolutionary events which unfolded in Crimea in 1917 were an outcome of the Russian Empire's increasing socioeconomic disparities compounded by its participation in World War I. While Crimea was not the site of any military campaigns, the war years, which began in the summer of 1914, did bring about changes that set the stage for an even greater revolutionary transformation of Russian imperial society between 1917 and 1920.

When war broke out in August 1914, the initial combatants were the Allies (Great Britain, France, and Russia) opposed by the Central Powers (Germany and Austria-Hungary). Ottoman Turkey was poised to join the Central Powers should Russia declare war. The Ottomans took the initiative by undertaking a naval attack in October 1914 against several Black Sea ports, including Sevastopol and Feodosiya in Crimea. This prompted a Russian declaration of war, which provided a convenient justification for the Ottoman sultan to declare, on 14 November, a Holy War (*jihad*) against all states engaged in war with

Turkey and its allies. Two other neighboring states eventually joined the conflict: Bulgaria (1915) on the side of the Central Powers, and Romania (1916) on the side of the Allies. Although Bulgaria and Romania played only a minor role in the war itself, both states included a Crimean Tatar diaspora population, which itself was encouraged to take sides in the conflict.

Following Ottoman Turkey's entry into the war, Crimea, because of its geographic location, was drawn into the sphere of the Russian-Ottoman front which was based farther east in the Caucasus region. Crimea henceforth served as a staging zone for tsarist troops who embarked from its ports toward the front in the Caucasus, as well as a place of refuge for soldiers wounded in battles along Russia's western borders and for Armenians and Greeks fleeing from massacres inflicted upon them within the Ottoman Empire. The war years also witnessed a sharp increase in surveillance by the tsarist secret police over any elements suspected of anti-state activity. Crimea's Tatars and Germans were

◀ Ant Etkenmen *(I Pledge), the Crimean Tatar national anthem approved by the Kurultay in 1991. Words by Noman Chelebi-Jihan; music by Kemil Karikov.*

especially suspect as potential agents of Russia's enemies, whether Ottoman Turkey or Germany.

It is certainly true that there was a long-standing sympathy on the part of Crimea's Tatars for their Islamic co-religionists and the Ottoman Empire, which ever since the loss of Crimean independence in 1783 had served as a refuge for hundreds of thousands of ex-iles. Nevertheless, the Crimean Tatars did not heed the call of the Ottoman sultan to join that state's Holy War; instead, for the most part they remained loyal to the Russian Empire. The leading Muslim cleric in Crimea, the *mufti* Adil Mirza Karashayskiy, issued a declaration of loyalty to Russia, which encouraged thousands of Crimean Tatars to volunteer for service in the tsarist army. There already existed the elite Crimean Cavalry Regiment, which gained a reputation as one of empire's best fighting units. Living up to its reputation, the Crimean Regiment served with distinction in battles along Russia's western borders, that is, what for the rest of Europe's combatants was known as the Eastern Front. Although there were no known desertions, some Crimean Tatars who found themselves as prisoners-of-war in Austria-Hungary did volunteer for service in the Ottoman Army.

Another component of the Crimean Tatar world was the prewar Vatan/Fatherland Society, the nationalist organization based in the Ottoman capital of Istanbul whose goal was independence for Crimea. The slow but steady return to Crimea of nationally conscious Tatar activists from Ottoman exile, which had

Seytjelil Hattat, Hasan Sabri Ayvazov, Noman Chelebi-Jihan, and Jafar Seydamet before the Khan's Palace in Bakhchysaray, 26 November/8 December 1917.

begun in 1908, was to continue even after the outbreak of World War I in 1914. Among the most prominent of these returnees were the founders of the Vatan Society, Noman Chelebi-Jihan and Jafar Seydamet, both of whom considered the outbreak of war as the first step toward the "impending revolution" in Russia. With these expectations in mind, they called on their followers to organize underground cells of the Vatan/Fatherland Society in most villages throughout Crimea. As part of the tsarist regime's tight control over suspicious anti-state elements, Chelebi-Jihan and Seydamet were drafted into the tsarist army. This turned out to be an advantage, since they simply continued their work, now in a military setting, and were able to transform many soldiers into nationally conscious patriots who one day might fight on behalf of the Crimean Tatar cause.

The year 1917 ushered in a new era in Crimean history: a four-year period marked by revolutionary upheaval, foreign invasion, and civil war. These developments began to unfold in February 1917 with the collapse of tsarist rule and its replacement by a Provisional Government which proclaimed as its goal the maintenance of a unified Russia and its transformation into a parliamentary democracy governed by a constitution. At the same time, councils (*soviets*) of workers and soldiers—to whom peasants were later added—were formed in various towns and cities, calling for radical social changes and an end to the war. Finally, there were other councils

which represented national groups and which proclaimed the establishment of autonomous and eventually independent states. Among the "national" councils were those which called for the creation of a Ukrainian state and a Crimean Tatar state.

All the aforementioned forces were present in Crimea: (1) the Provisional Government and other forces which tried to maintain a unified Russia; (2) the soviets of workers', soldiers', and peasants' "deputies," which eventually became the instrument of the Communist-oriented Bolshevik party and its utopian goal to create the world's first worker's state; and (3) Tatar nationalists hoping to create their own independent state based in Crimea. During the next several months, each of these contenders for power tried to garner support for its cause. Those hoping to live in a non-Bolshevik Russia looked to the armies of the so-called Whites; the soviets to Bolshevik Russia; and the Crimean Tatar nationalists to the Central Powers—Germany or, preferably, its ally Ottoman Turkey.

Immediately following the Revolution of February 1917 that ended tsarist rule, Russia's new Provisional Government based in the former imperial capital of St. Petersburg, renamed Petrograd, tried to establish its authority in Crimea by working with former tsarist officials and the established socially conservative elements (aristocratic landowners, businessmen, and clerics), both Slavic and Crimean Tatar. The Provisional Government was not, however, favorably inclined to ideas of territorial autonomy and certainly not independence for a Crimean Tatar state. Meanwhile, younger Crimean Tatar national activists with ties to the Istanbul-based émigré Vatan Society convoked in Simferopol in March 1917 the All-Crimean Muslim Congress. Most of the delegates came from the society's underground cells which were set up throughout Crimea during the war years.

The congress formed a Provisional Crimean Muslim Executive Committee, whose leading members were Noman Chelebi-Jihan and Jafar Seydamet, both of whom had just returned home from service in the tsarist army. Chelebi-Jihan also took up the post of *mufti*, the highest Muslim clerical office in Crimea, whose holder was for the first time chosen by democratic vote at the congress. A few months later, in the summer of 1917, the leaders of the Central Executive Council created a Crimean Tatar political party, Milli Firka. The party was both nationalist and socialist in orientation, calling for the break-up of the large estates held by private landowners and by the church. The nationalist leaders were determined to replace the Muslim clergy as the leading force in Crimean Tatar society. This was not an easy task, however, since the conservative clerics (Muslim and Orthodox), together with Crimea's Russian and Tatar large landowners (*pomeshchiks*), continued to be recognized by the Provisional Government in Petrograd.

The attitude of the Provisional Government soon became a moot issue, however, because on 7 November 1917 it was overthrown and replaced by a Soviet government under the Bolshevik leader Vladimir Lenin. These

First meeting of the Crimean Tatar National Assembly (Kurultay), Bakhchysaray, 26 November 8 December. 1917.

The tamgha, *golden seal of the Crimean Khanate, later adopted as a symbol of independent statehood by Crimean Tatar nationalists; and the pan-Turkic turquoise colored flag of the Crimean National Republic.*

changed circumstances provided an opening for the Crimean Muslim Central Executive Committee, which, together with the Milli Firka party, made plans to convene a national assembly, or Kurultay (the historic name for the gathering of tribal leaders that for centuries had chosen Crimea's khans). On 26 November/8 December 1917, the Crimean Tatar Kurultay was held on the historic grounds of the former palace of the khans, in Bakhchysaray. The Kurultay elected a five-member Crimean Tatar government, or National Directorate, to be based in Simferopol and headed by Chelebi-Jihan and Seydamet. Before the end of 1917, a constitution was adopted which declared the formation of an independent Crimean People's Republic (25 December). The new government gained control of the Crimean Cavalry Regiment, which in the interim was demobilized from the tsarist army. The Directorate also began to negotiate with the Ottoman Empire in the hope of gaining support for the fledging Crimean Tatar state.

Just before the Crimean Tatars convened their Kurultay, local Russian, Ukrainian, and Crimean Tatar activists of various political persuasions organized elections to yet another body, the Crimean Provincial Assembly. Hence, before the end of 1917 there were two governments based in Simferopol: the National Directorate of the Crimean People's Republic supporting the idea of an independent Crimean Tatar state; and the Crimean Provincial Assembly remaining loyal to the idea of a unified democratic Russia. The third—and for the moment dominant political force—were the soviets loyal to the Bolshevik government in Petrograd. In Crimea, the most important of these was the Sevastopol Soviet, which in mid-December 1917 established a Military-Revolutionary Committee (Revkom) for the entire Taurida province. In cooperation with sailors from the Black Sea Fleet, who in June 1917 had rebelled and eliminated their officers, the Military-Revolutionary Committee set out to establish its authority throughout the peninsula. The brutal manner in which the naval officers were killed the previous summer (by drowning in the harbor of Sevastopol) set the tone for what was to become standard Bolshevik terror tactics against all their enemies in the months and years to come. By the first week of January 1918, aside from Sevastopol, the

Typical political demonstration in revolutionary era Crimea, Nakhimov Square in Sevastopol, 6 October 1917.

The bodies of White Russian Army officers executed on the "Night of St. Bartholomew," put on display along the shore at Yevpatoriya, summer of 1918.

port cities of Feodosiya and Kerch were in Bolshevik hands.

For their part, the members of the Crimean Tatar National Directorate were divided over how to deal with the Bolshevik challenge. Some (led by Chelebi-Jihan) favored cooperation, while others (led by Seydamet) were opposed. On the other hand, the Crimean Tatar government did reach an accord with the Central Rada of the Ukrainian National Republic, something that only further exacerbated the situation in the eyes of the Bolshevik Military-Revolutionary Committee in Sevastopol.

Consequently, in January 1918, Bolshevik-led sailors and marines from the Black Sea fleet marched northward to Simferopol, where they dispersed both the Crimean People's Republic's National Directorate and the multi-party democratically oriented Crimean Provincial Assembly. The Military-Revolutionary Committee then convened a conference in Sevastopol (28-30 January), which, in turn, created a governing council of Taurida province. It immediately rejected the claims of the Central Rada in Kyiv—which in the interim (22 January) had proclaimed an independent state—to incorporate Crimea and the Black Sea Fleet into Ukraine.

As part of its campaign throughout February and March 1918, soldiers and sailors nominally under the control of Taurida Military-Revolutionary Committee based in Sevastopol spread terror throughout Crimea's towns and countryside, killing thousands of Tatar nationalists, Muslim and Christian clergy, wealthy landowners, and non-Bolshevik Russian and Ukrainian "bourgeois counter-revolutionaries." To drive home their point, the Bolsheviks captured and killed the very Crimean Tatar leader who favored some kind of political rapprochement, the president of the Kurultay, Noman Chelebi-Jihan. That act unwittingly transformed him into a national martyr. Ever since then Chelebi-Jihan has been remembered as the ultimate patriot whose love for his country is embodied in poetic verses he wrote and which were adopted as the Crimean Tatar national anthem, "Ant Etkenmen" (I Pledge).

Flushed with a sense of success brought about by this first terror operation, the Bolshevik-led Sevastopol Military-Revolutionary Committee proclaimed in March 1918 the formation of the Taurida Soviet Socialist Republic, whose territory was to be limited to the Crimean peninsula. The soviet republic was short-lived, however, lasting little more than a month. The reason for its failure had to do with monumental changes on the international scene, which were to have a direct impact on Crimea.

Already at the end of 1917, Bolshevik Russia withdrew from the war and in early March 1918 signed a peace treaty at Brest-Litovsk with the leading Central Powers, Germany and Austria-Hungary. Among the treaty's provisions was recognition of Ukraine as an independent state under the auspices of the Central Rada based in Kyiv. The Central Rada welcomed troops from Germany and Austria-Hungary to help protect Ukraine's newly acquired independence.

Members of the Council of People's Commissars
of the Taurida Soviet Socialist Republic, spring 1918.

87

Matwiej Sulejman Sulkiewicz
(1865-1920).

In these new circumstances, a delegation of Crimean Tatar leaders went to Germany with the request that that country consider making Crimea a part of its sphere of interest. The Germans responded by dispatching an army, which in April 1918 marched southward from Ukraine through the isthmus of Perekop. Together with the German forces was a Muslim Corps comprised of Crimean Tatar exiles from the Dobruja region of Romania, who were commanded by a Tatar from Lithuania, the former tsarist general, Matwiej Sulejman Sulkiewicz. Although the treaty with the Central Powers recognizing independent Ukraine did not include Crimea, the Central Rada in Kyiv nonetheless claimed the region

and sent a brigade under Colonel Petro Bolbochan, which entered northern Crimea before the German advance. Such token interference on the part of the Ukrainian Central Rada was not tolerated by the German military, which considered Crimea exclusively within its occupation zone. While the Germans forced Bolbochan's Ukrainian brigade to leave Crimea, they did employ Sulkiewicz's Muslim Corps to help clear the region of Bolshevik forces. They were successful, so that by the second half of April the Taurida Soviet Republic ceased to exist. Its entire government leadership was caught by Russian and Tatar units fighting alongside the German Army and summarily executed near Yalta.

The Crimean Tatar leadership welcomed the arrival of the Germans and, in return, they were allowed to restore the Kurultay but not their own national government. Instead, a Crimean Regional Government was formed in June 1918 as a client state of Germany and headed by General Sulkiewicz. Sulkiewicz's government was not sympathetic to Crimean Tatar political and socioeconomic needs; in any case, his rule came to an abrupt end when the Germans returned home following the armistice of November 1918 that ended World War I.

The last phase of the revolutionary and civil war era in Crimea encompassed the years 1919 and most of 1920. This was an incredibly complex period during which attempts to continue Crimean Tatar nationalist rule

*Flag of the Crimean Regional
Government under Sulkiewicz (1918)
with the coat of arms of the former
Russian imperial province of Taurida.*

were challenged by pro-Russian forces, whether the anti-Bolshevik conservative Whites, or the Bolshevik Reds in alliance with Soviet Russia. The least effective of these alternatives was the administration that succeeded General Sulkiewicz. Functioning from November 1918 to April 1919, it was headed by Solomon Krym, a Karaite and wealthy Crimean landowner. In contrast to the pro-German orientation of his predecessor, the Crimean Regional Government under Krym was supported by White Russian forces led by General Anton Denikin. Accepting the White general's view of a "Russia one and indivisible," Krym hoped that a future Russian government would evolve along the lines of western European liberal democratic states.

The authority of the Crimean Regional Government was undermined by partisan units allied with the Bolsheviks and by the arrival in early April 1919 of Red Army forces from the north. Before the end of the month, local Bolshevik party activists met in Simferopol (29 April) to proclaim the Crimean Soviet Socialist Republic headed by Lenin's brother, Dmitriy Ulyanov. But by early July this entity collapsed following the return to Crimea of General Denikin's White Russian armies together with thousands of anti-Bolshevik refugees. By this time the cause of the Whites was in rapid decline throughout most of Russia, so that Denikin hoped to transform the Crimea into an "island bastion" of anti-Communism. Should he succeed, it would be a purely "Russian bastion," and with that in mind the White forces showed no tolerance for the Crimean Tatars or for any of their political demands. Therefore, for the remainder of 1919 Denikin engaged in a systematic policy of repression against Crimean Tatar activists. In response, many Crimean Tatars in the Milli Firka nationalist party joined guerrilla units known as "green bands"

*Solomon Krym
(1867-1936).*

to fight against the Whites. Whereas some Milli Firkists (Jafar Seydamet) remained adamantly opposed to Russian rule, whether White or Red, the leftists in the party (Veli Ibrahimov) favored an alliance with the Bolsheviks in common cause against the Whites. An alliance was struck but did not last long.

At the outset of 1920 Denikin was replaced by another White general, Baron Pyotr Wrangel. He attempted to correct the mistakes of his predecessor and to respond positively to the cultural needs of the Crimean Tatars and the demands of the peasantry for land reform. But the days of the Whites were clearly numbered. During the first week of November 1920, Bolshevik forces along the Red Army's Southern Front commanded by Mikhail Frunze breached the defences across the Perekop isthmus and farther east crossed the shallow half-frozen waters of the narrow Chongar Strait which gave them access to the heart of the Crimea. This forced the rapid retreat southward of the White forces, and that, in turn, set off a massive evacuation of anti-Bolshevik refugees from the coastal ports of Kerch, Feodosiya, and finally Sevastopol. More than 145,000 people, nearly half of whom were White army soldiers and personnel, crowded onto 120 ships which set sail across the Black Sea.[1] Most of the human cargo that disembarked at Constantinople eventually dispersed to various capitals throughout Europe, from Belgrade to Prague, Berlin, and

General Pyotr Wrangel (first row, third from the left) together with White Russian military commanders and members of the Government of South Russia, in Sevastopol, July 1920.

Evacuation of the White Russian troops from Crimea, 1920.

especially Paris. Some found safe haven as far away as North and South America, Australia, even the Fiji Islands.

The evacuation hastily put together under the protection of the French navy (based at the time in Odessa) ended on 14 November 1920, when the last cruiser, with the White General Wrangel on board, departed from Sevastopol. As the overcrowded ships pulled away from the shore, the last view that their frightened passengers, now refugees, were ever to have of their beloved "Russian homeland" took the form of flickering and slowly fading lights along the coasts of Crimea.

Chapter 7

The Crimean Autonomous Soviet Socialist Republic

The return of Soviet rule to Crimea—for the third and last time—began on an ominous note. In many ways, the exiled White refugees were the lucky ones. The more than 52,000 White soldiers and officers imprisoned during the Red Army offensive in 1919-1920, as well as the civilian population of Crimea were left defenceless against the Bolsheviks and all those who cooperated with the new regime. For a full year beginning in mid-November 1920, Crimea was placed under the authority of the Crimean Revolutionary Committee (Krymrevkom), led by Béla Kun. This was the same Béla Kun who headed Hungary's Soviet Republic until it collapsed in August 1919. The disgraced Kun fled to Soviet Russia, where the following year he was appointed to the Military Council of the Red Army's Southern Front. As the Bolsheviks were advancing toward the peninsula in October 1920, Kun already predicted that "Crimea is like a bottle from which not a single counter-revolutionary will escape."[1]

Kun seemed determined to make up for the defeat of the Bolshevik revolution in his native Hungary by taking revenge on Crimea. Within the course of one fateful year, beginning in November 1920 and coinciding with the period of War Communism already underway in the rest of the Soviet state, anywhere from 50,000 to 100,000 real or suspected opponents of Soviet rule (including the Tatar "bourgeoisie," clergy, supporters of the now outlawed Milli Firka national party, and White officers left behind) were murdered—and often in the most brutal fashion—by decapitation, quartering, the hanging of women, children, and the elderly, and even the execution of wounded lying in hospitals.

Revolutionary justice was only one way in which the peninsula's inhabitants were forced into submission. Nearly five years of revolutionary upheaval and civil war (1917-1921) devastated Crimea's industrial enterprises (based in Sevastopol and Kerch) and its agricultural sector, in particular the formerly highly productive orchards and vineyards confiscated by various regimes during the revolution-

◄ *Mass terror against all enemies of the revolution was characteristic of Bolshevik rule when it reached Crimea. The banner reads: Death to the Bourgeoisie and their Lackies. Long Live the Red Terror!!*

Béla Kun (1886-1938) and the brutal interrogator Zemlyachka—Rozaliya Zalkind (1876-1947), the main perpetrators of the year-long Bolshevik Red terror in Crimea from November 1920.

ary era from the large, privately owned landed estates which were left to decay. In contrast to Bolshevik promises, those estates were not divided and distributed to the landless peasantry. Instead, they were transformed into gigantic Soviet-style state farms (*sovkhozy*), which by the spring of 1921 already accounted for 25 percent of all arable land and 45 percent of all orchards and vineyards. If that were not enough, the political and socioeconomic disruptions were accompanied by a severe drought in the summer of 1921 and the beginnings of a famine, which by the outset of the following year had struck between 60 to 70 percent of the population. Consequently, between the years 1921 and 1923 an estimated 100,000 to 110,000 residents of Crimea died from starvation or related diseases. The famine hit especially hard the mountainous regions and northern steppelands where the vast majority of the inhabitants were Crimean Tatars.[2]

In early 1921, the Soviet leadership in Moscow, which was becoming increasingly concerned about the ongoing opposition to Bolshevik rule in Crimea, sent its specialist on Muslim questions, Mirsaid Sultan-Galiev (himself a Volga Tatar), to investigate. Sultan-Galiev submitted a report that strongly criticized the draconian rule of the Béla Kun-led Revolutionary Committee and the ineffectiveness of Crimea's local Communist party leadership. The report called for the creation of an autonomous republic, the end to the radical land reform policies, and the introduction of measures to attract Crimean Tatars to join the Communist party. All of the recommendations were accepted by the Bolshevik central government in Moscow and were expected to be carried out by local party activists in Crimea. Like other Bolshevik leaders at the time, Sultan-Galiev believed that a Soviet republic with a substantial number of Crimean Tatars among its officials would serve as a beacon of the proletarian revolution

Yearly set of bread ration cards for children aged 5 to 16 during the 1921-1923 famine in Crimea.

for Turkey and other lands in the East.

In early November 1921, the Constituent Congress of Crimea's Council (Soviet) of Workers', Peasants', Soldiers' and Black Sea Fleet Deputies called into being the Crimean Autonomous Socialist Soviet Republic (the Crimean ASSR). The Constituent Assembly adopted a constitution for the autonomous Crimean republic, and before disbanding it elected the Crimean Central Executive Committee with a government based in Simferopol to be administered by a five-member presidium and fifteen-member Council of People's Commissars. The new republic was not, however, placed within the jurisdiction of the territorially adjacent Soviet Ukraine, but rather within the Russian Federated Soviet Socialist Republic.

This marked the dawn of a new era in the history of Crimea. It is true that the region had its own autonomous republic, an entity that responded to the Soviet practice of creating nationality-based territorial administrative units. The question

remained, however, as to what degree, if any, the republic would be Tatar in nature.

Despite Crimea's centuries-long association with the Tatars, by the 1920s they actually made up only one-quarter of the region's population (see Table 7.1). And although they were not considered the republic's titular nationality, the Crimean Tatars did, at least initially, become the dominant political and socioeconomic force in the Crimean ASSR. For instance, individuals were given leadership positions in local town administrations, factories, and collective and state farms, while as a group they were assigned the largest number of self-governing village soviets: 144 Crimean Tatar as compared to 106 for the Russians and only 3 for Ukrainians.[3]

TABLE 7.1

Nationality composition of the Crimean ASSR, 1926[4]

Nationality	Number	Percentage
Russians	301,000	42.2
Crimean Tatars	179,000	25.1
Ukrainians	77,000	10.8
Germans	44,000	6.1
Jews (Ashkenazim)	40,000	5.6
Greeks	16,000	2.3
Bulgarians	11,000	1.6
Armenians	11,000	1.5
Karaites	8,000	1.1
Jews (Krymchaks)	6,000	0.8
Others	20,000	2.8
TOTAL	**714,000**	**99.9**

95

MAP 9

CRIMEAN AUTONOMOUS SOVIET SOCIALIST REPUBLIC, ca. 1930

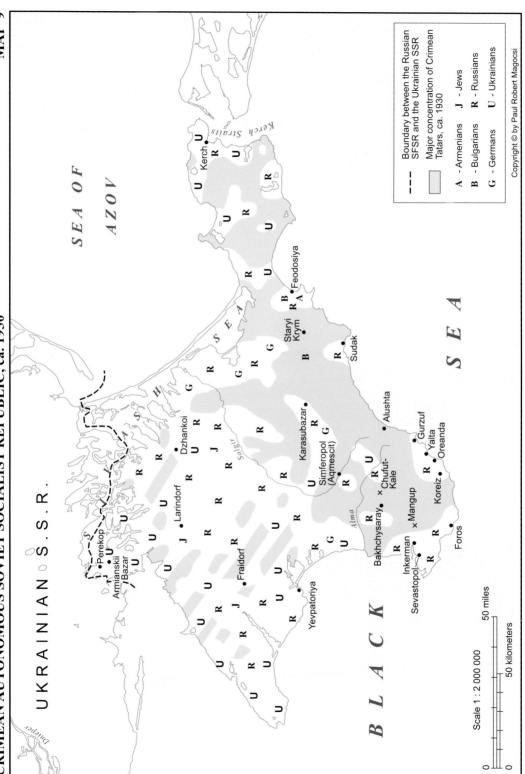

UKRAINIAN S.S.R.

SEA OF AZOV

Kerch Straits

Dnieper

Perekop
Armianskii
Bazar
Larindorf
Dzhankoi
Fraidorf
Yevpatoriya

Salgir

Karasubazar
Simferopol (Aqmescit)
Chufut-Kale
Bakhchysaray × Mangup
Inkerman
Sevastopol
Foros
Koreiz
Oreanda
Yalta
Gurzuf
Alushta
Sudak
Staryi Krym
Feodosiya

Alma

BLACK SEA

Boundary between the Russian SFSR and the Ukrainian SSR

Major concentration of Crimean Tatars, ca. 1930

A - Armenians   J - Jews
B - Bulgarians   R - Russians
G - Germans   U - Ukrainians

Copyright © by Paul Robert Magocsi

Scale 1 : 2 000 000

0   50 miles
0   50 kilometers

It is perhaps not surprising, considering the historic record of Tatar-Slavic relations, that the leadership role enjoyed in the 1920s by the Crimean Tatars in many facets of public life caused resentment among the local Russians and Ukrainians, who together comprised over half of the population of the autonomous republic. Crimea's government even attempted to stop the ongoing influx of Russian, Ukrainian, and Jewish settlers from other parts of the Soviet Union, who were being encouraged by the central government in Moscow to participate in the reconstruction of Crimea. The local authorities in Simferopol viewed these settlers as a threat to their own goal of trying to "re-Tatarize" Crimea, most especially the peninsula's lowland steppe. In a further effort to reverse what was (from the Crimean Tatar perspective) a demographic imbalance, Tatars who had fled mostly to Turkey during Russia's Civil War and the initial period of Soviet rule (1919-1921) were granted amnesty and encouraged to return home. It is therefore not surprising that for subsequent generations of Crimean Tatars the five-year period, 1923 to 1928, was to be remembered as the "golden age" of Soviet Crimea.

The golden age, albeit short-lived, was in large part due to the activity of Veli Ibrahimov, a former member of the Crimean Tatar National party (Milli Firka), who by 1920 had become a committed Bolshevik and nationalist-Communist. Moscow entrusted Ibrahimov with the political and social reconstruction of Crimea, which during the period of War Communism and the accompanying famine (1921-1923) had

Veli Ibrahimov (1888-1928), seated in the center among the members of the Presidium of the Central Executive Committee of the Crimean ASSR.

suffered an overall twenty-one percent loss in its population. As chairman of both Crimea's Communist party Central Committee and its government's Council of People's Commissars, Ibrahimov oversaw the introduction of the New Economic Policy (NEP). This meant that the next several years were characterized by a temporary return to a semi-market-driven economy and, on the political and cultural front, by Tatarization, the local version of the all-Soviet policy of indigenization (*korenizatsiia*).

Ibrahimov achieved his goals in several ways. As part of the policy of indigenization, he brought Tatars into all levels of the Crimean ASSR administration. Within a few years, Crimean

Recently erected monument in Bilohirsk/Karasubazar to the town's native son, the Crimean Tatar writer Bekir Chobanzade (1893-1937).

Tatars (who still comprised only 25 percent of the population) made up from 30 to 60 percent of the membership in governmental and party organs. Most of the new officials were, like Ibrahimov himself, former members of Milli Firka, the revolutionary era non-Communist Crimean Tatar nationalist party outlawed in 1921. In the economic sphere, he overturned the radical changes introduced during the period of War Communism by facilitating the return of land to its former owners, in particular Crimean Tatar peasant villagers, and by limiting government interference in the operation of industrial enterprises, albeit under the management of inexperienced Crimean Tatar appointees. Finally, in the cultural sphere, he promoted the policy of Tatarization.

Tatarization took different forms. Elementary schools were established (387 by 1930), in which the Crimean Tatar language (still using the Arabic alphabet) was made the language of instruction.[5] The very question of what the Crimean Tatar literary language was—or should be—was finally resolved. Soviet linguists, together with the Crimean Tatar writer Bekir Chobanzade created a common Crimean Tatar grammar based on the peninsula's central mountain dialect, which had evolved during the era of the Crimean Khanate. This approach was called the *Orta Yolak*, or Middle Road; that is, the codification of a common Crimean Tatar language based on the hybrid of Kipchak Turkic and Oghuz (the core of modern Turkish), which had become the spoken language of the majority of the Crimean Tatars. Four teacher's colleges were set up (in Feodosiya, Bakhchysaray, Yalta, and Simferopol) to train instructors in the new literary language.

In the autonomous republic's capital city, Simferopol (now also called by its historic Tatar name: Aq-Mescit, pronounced Akmesjit), Taurida University was opened in 1918, already before the onset of Soviet rule. The authorities of the Crimean ASSR set out to expand the scope of the institution. Of particular importance for Crimean Tatar nationality-building was the university's Turkic-Tatar Department and from 1925 its Crimean Pedagogical Institute, which trained a large number of teachers and scholars (anthropologists and linguists). They set out to record systematically the Crimean Tatar cultural heritage (language, folklore, music) and, with the support of the central Soviet research institutions in Moscow, carried out extensive archaeological research at pre-historic and medieval sites throughout the peninsula. At the same time, the Crimean State Publishing House was set up to make available scholarly studies and literary works in the Crimean Tatar language.

The resultant wide range of published scholarship contributed to a revised understanding of the ethnogenesis of the Crimean Tatar people. No longer were they associated solely with the Mongolo-Tatar nomadic invaders and the Turkic Kipchak warrior steppe peoples; rather, they were presented as an ethnic amalgam descended from the Scythians,

Kerch. Voikov Metallurgical Factory, 1930s.

Sarmatians, Alans, and coastal Greeks, who together with the Kipchak nomads formed a unique Crimean Tatar ethnos. Not only were the Crimean Tatars different from other Turkic-speaking peoples, even more importantly they were considered the indigenous inhabitants who, therefore, had a historic right to the Crimean peninsula.

The year 1928 brought profound changes to Crimea as it did to the Soviet Union as a whole. In that year the central Soviet government in Moscow, under the leadership of Joseph Stalin, the chairman of the All-Union Communist party, introduced the concept of a planned command economy. As a result of the so-called Stalinist revolution, all decisions regarding economic policy

Dzhankoi. Electro-energy station, built in the 1930s.

and development were henceforth to be made by the State Planning Commission (Gosplan) based in Moscow and implemented according to its guidelines throughout the Soviet Union, which henceforth was treated as a single economic unit. This comprehensive, supposedly more rational approach meant an immediate end to the NEP and its tolerance of small-scale privately owned businesses and market economy. In its stead, the First Five-Year Plan was introduced, setting for all aspects of Soviet agriculture and especially of industry production schedules and goals which were to be fulfilled at the end of each five-year period.

The first, second, and third five-year plans were introduced into the Crimean ASSR. As part of the plans devised in Moscow, new industrial enterprises were established in Simferopol (machine tool, clothing, and food-processing plants), Sevastopol (machine-building and ship-building shops), and Kerch (steel mills and chemical factories) with its nearby Komysh-Buruny Iron Ore Complex to extract and process industrial metals and limestone. To power Crimea's expanding industrial base an electro-energy station was built at Dzhankoi.

Both before and after the introduction of the planned economy in 1928, the Soviet authorities introduced policies to improve the educational standards of Crimea's inhabitants and to develop further the region's unique natural resource—its mild climate. The educational infrastructure was transformed with the opening of hundreds of elementary schools, libraries, and adult-education classes, with the result that by 1934 over 97 percent of the population was literate.[6]

Aside from the already existing Taurida University in Simferopol, the Soviet regime established in the Crimean ASSR four other university-level institutions as well as 40 technical colleges (each with a teacher's college attached), worker's colleges (9), and scholarly research institutes (19).[7] Capitalizing on Crimea's best known resource, the Soviet authorities undertook to restore and expand sanatoria and other health facilities by taking over prewar establishments, building new ones, and transforming the elegant nineteenth-century aristocratic and imperial palaces into resort residences for workers and, most especially for the upper echelons (*nomenklatura*) of the Communist party ruling elite and their world-wide "comrades" associated with the Communist International (Comintern). For example, the very same Béla Kun who had wrought such destruction on the population of Crimea during the revolutionary-era Bolshevik terror, was

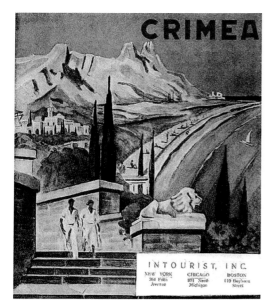

Poster (1930s) of Intourist, the Soviet state travel agency, advertising Crimea to potential American visitors.

who actively supported—or who somehow accommodated to—the ideological needs of the world's first worker's state. Crimean themes enriched the corpus of Soviet Russian literature through the works of Sergei Sergeev-Tsenskiy, Alexander Grin, Konstantin Trenëv, and Maximilian Voloshin, who, through the Union of Writers of Crimea, encountered renowned fellow authors—Maxim Gorky and Vladimir Mayakovsky, among others—on their frequent visits to the region. Crimea was also the home of and source of inspiration for the Soviet Union's most popular painter of monumental historical scenes, the Ukrainian Mykola Samokysh, and the native and lifelong resident of Feodosyia, best known for his romanticized landscapes,

on more than one occasion able to enjoy pleasurable stays at the former Yusupov palace in Koreyiz. It was not long before Crimea came to be known as the *Vsesoyuznaya zdravnitsa*—the health resort for the entire Soviet Union.

As in nineteenth-century imperial Russia, so too did the Crimean ASSR become a destination for creative artists from various parts of the Soviet Union

Koreyiz.
The former Yusupov Palace designed by Nikolai Krasnov, built in 1909, reserved for foreign guests and officials of the Communist International in the 1920s and 1930s.

Tobacco plantation in Crimea (1930s).

The new technology on a cooperative farm/
kolkhoz *in Crimea (1929).*

Konstantin Bogaevskiy.

The Stalinist "revolution from above" initiated in 1928 also had a profound—and, as it turned out, a negative—impact on Crimean Tatar cultural and social life, in particular the program of Tatarization. Already in January of that fateful year, the Crimean ASSR Communist party and government leader Veli Ibrahimov was arrested, os-

tensibly for disagreeing with Moscow's decision to settle Jews from Belarus in Crimea. The question of Jews in Crimea and the defense of their interests by the Soviet authorities was, of course, only an excuse. Nevertheless, it proved be a convenient excuse to get rid of an unwanted nationalist leader. Four months later, Ibrahimov was executed on charges of bourgeois nationalism, and his policies and programs totally repudiated. The regimentation connected with the Stalinist revolution that eventually affected all walks of life started, in effect, earlier in the Crimean ASSR than in other parts of the Soviet Union. The results, however, were the same.

In the agricultural sector, collectivization was the goal; that is, to replace privately owned landholdings with collective (*kolkhoz*) and state (*sovkhoz*) farms. Communist officials argued that collectivization would make the agricultural sector more efficient and productive. Actually, in the 1920s, nearly eight percent of Crimea's arable land (the highest percentage in the entire Soviet Union) was transferred to collectives by the peasants themselves—on a voluntary basis.[8] But Stalin was displeased with those results, and in late 1927 he introduced throughout the entire Soviet Union a policy of forced collectivization. Everyone was expected to accept the wisdom of Communist party decisions, and peasants in particular would have been well aware of the popular saying of the time: "He who is against the collective is against Soviet rule." In the interest of the greater good of society, the state felt obliged to act against those who were opposed to collectivization, beginning with the relatively wealthier peasants dubbed *kulaks*. In 1928-1929, during a process known as dekulakization, between 35,000 and 40,000 of the more efficient and productive agriculturalists were driven out of Crimea and exiled to Soviet Central Asia.[9]

Forced collectivization took several years to complete (October 1927 through 1931), largely because small-scale Crimean Tatar and other peasants expressed their displeasure with the loss of their land by refusing to sow crops, by killing their livestock instead of turning them over to state and collective forms, and by attacking state officials and property, including at least one major uprising (at Alakat in December 1930). Such disruptive factors resulted in great hardship and food shortages in the early 1930s, although the Crimean ASSR did not experience in any way the degree of famine and death occurring during those same years in neighboring Soviet Ukraine's

Soviet postage stamp (1933) depicting the Tatars of Crimea, design by the artist Vasiliy Zavyalov.

Holodomor (death by famine).

Actually, by the second half of the 1930s, Crimea's agricultural sector recovered, so that production levels in some categories (grain, fruits, vineyards) were nearly double what they had been before World War I. Although most of Crimea's agriculture was now carried out in village-based collective farms, it was state farms that dominated the increasingly successful wine and tobacco industries.

The downfall of the Crimean Communist party leader Ibrahimov in 1928 was soon followed by a wide-scale purge from government, schools, and other institutions of all Crimean Tatars suspected of being "tinged with Veli Ibrahimovism." Upwards of 3,500 Crimean Tatar government and party officials and intellectuals (including the popular writers Bekir Chobanzade and Shevki Bektöre) were arrested and either imprisoned, exiled, or executed.[10] Also between 1931 and 1935 the religious facet of Crimean Tatar identity was virtually eliminated with the closure of hundreds of mosques and the exile to Siberia of most of the peninsula's Muslim clergy (*mullahs*). Having removed Crimean Tatars from positions of authority, the Soviet security forces (NKVD) undertook further purges, so that between 1935 and 1937 over three thousand persons were arrested and nearly 400 alleged espionage, "diversionist," "counter-revolutionary," and "Fascist-German" groups destroyed.[11]

In an effort to distance the Crimean Tatars even further from their traditional heritage and to bring them more in

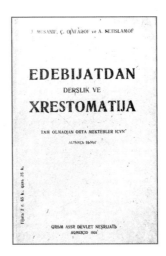

Children's books from 1920s and 1930s depicting the change of alphabets imposed on the Crimean Tatar language: Arabic, Roman/Latin, and Cyrillic.

line with modern socialist currents, the very face of their language was changed. Beginning as early as 1922, a series of meetings was held among the various Turkic-speaking peoples of the Soviet Union to promote the idea of replacing the traditional Arabic alphabet with the Roman (Latin) alphabet. At the time, some of the leading Crimean Tatar intellectuals and political leaders (Bekir Chobanzade, Veli Ibrahimov, and others) were opposed to the alphabet change. In response, the Soviet authorities accused the supporters of the Arabic alphabet of "bourgeois nationalism" and of holding anti-progressive views, and in 1929 they simply decreed that Crimean Tatar publications and public signage must henceforth be in the Roman/Latin alphabet. No sooner had that change been implemented than a few years later the Soviet authorities changed their views again, and in 1938 ordered the replacement of the Roman alphabet with the Cyrillic alphabet. In effect, all the achievements of the Tatarization program led by Veli Ibrahimov until 1928 had been effectively dismantled. One could, therefore, easily conclude that during the 1930s the Tatars were being subjected to a state-imposed policy of cultural genocide, with the result that Crimea was rapidly transformed into a Slavic, or more specifically a Sovietized Russian land.

Jews and Karaites

Crimea differs from most other lands in central and eastern Europe in that it has three rather distinct communities of Jewish tradition: Krymchaks, Ashkenazim, and Karaites. The Krymchaks and Ashkenazim are both Rabbinite, and as such accept the authority of Talmudic law. They differ, however, with regard to their origins and time of settlement in Crimea.

The Krymchaks are considered indigenous to the peninsula. Their very name, meaning "inhabitant of Crimea," was introduced in the 1780s by the Russian imperial government to distinguish them from other peoples of Jewish tradition. They are the descendents of Hellenized Jews who first settled in Crimea during the first century BCE and whose numbers were supplemented in the seventh century CE by immigrants from the Byzantine Empire. They lived primarily in the Mongol administrative center of Solkhat/Staryi Krym, in the mountain-top cave towns of Kirk-Yer/Chufut Kale and Mangup, and in Venetian- and Genoese-controlled coastal cities, in particular Caffa/Feodosiya, which became an early center of Crimean rabbinite Jewish life. From the sixteenth century, Karasubazar/Bilohirsk gradually became the main center of the Krymchaks. It was also at this time that the Crimean Tatar language, written in Hebrew characters, was adopted as their spoken and written language. The resultant Judeo-Crimean Tatar language was to remain in use until the twentieth century, and it even became the language of instruction in some elementary schools and adult literacy classes during the early Soviet period. The number of Krymchaks was always very small, with only about 3,500 recorded in 1897 and 6,500 on the eve of World War II and the Holocaust.

More numerous were the Ashkenazim. They were Yiddish-speaking Jews from the western regions of the Russian Empire; that is, from the so-called Pale of Settlement, which was annexed from the Polish-Lithuanian Commonwealth at the end of the eighteenth century. The Ashkenazim were among the various peoples invited by the imperial authorities to settle in Crimea, and by 1881 they numbered about 10,000. In the wake of pogroms occurring at that time in certain areas of the Pale, many more fled to Crimea and by 1897 they numbered over 25,000. They were concentrated in Crimea's urban areas, with over 80 percent living in four cities: Simferopol, Kerch, Sevastopol, and Feodosiya.

In-migration of Ashkenazic Jews continued during the interwar years of the twentieth century, when various Jewish organizations actively supported agricultural settlement. After 1924, the Soviet government itself initiated a large-scale settlement project for Jews primarily within southern Ukraine and Crimea. Some Soviet Jewish leaders felt that Crimea might even become the site of a Jewish Soviet Socialist Republic. Although during the 1920s over 5,100 Jewish families were settled primarily in Crimea's northern lowland steppe zone, where two nationality districts (Fraidorf and Larindorf) were established, the peninsula proved unsuitable for any massive resettlement of the millions of Jews from the western regions of the Soviet Union. Moreover, when forced collectivization of agriculture was introduced in the early 1930s, many Jews abandoned the agricultural settlements. Nevertheless, at the outbreak of World War II, there were about 60,000 Ashkenazic Jews living in Crimea's urban and rural areas.

With the invasion by Nazi Germany and occupation of Crimea that began in the late fall of 1941, those Jews (primarily Ashkenazim) who did not succeed in fleeing eastward with the retreating Soviet forces were systematically liquidated. Already by April 1942 the German authorities could proudly declare that Crimea was Judenrein (cleansed of Jews). Toward the end of the war, Soviet Jewish activists led by the actor Solomon Michoels revived the idea of Crimea as a possible Soviet Jewish republic and homeland for all Soviet Jews who had moved eastward before the German advance and, therefore, survived the Holocaust. The idea of Crimea in the guise of what some called a "Jewish California" was even discussed with American Jewish organizations, something that was possible at least while the Soviet Union had been an ally of the United States. But the supreme Soviet ruler, Joseph Stalin, in contrast to what had been promoted in the 1920s, opposed any large-scale Jewish settlement in Crimea and forbade any discussion of the topic with the Americans at the 1945 Yalta Conference.

Nevertheless, what came to be known as the "Crimean affair" was used by Stalin after 1948 to denounce all those who had favored a Soviet Jewish republic. This was part of a general campaign launched by the Soviet leader against all those whom he considered political enemies, many of whom were of Jewish descent or who were somehow connected with Jews. While Crimea never became a Soviet Jewish republic, it did become the postwar home for some Soviet Jews (mostly Ashkenazim), whose number reached over 26,000 according to the census of 1959.

The Karaites, also known as Karaim, are a Jewish sect whose origins are unclear and disputed. It is generally assumed that the sect was founded in the eighth century in Baghdad, and from there it spread throughout the Middle East. In the twelfth century, some Karaites settled in the Byzantine Empire (primarily in Constantinople and western Anatolia); from there they migrated to Crimea beginning in the mid-thirteenth century.

The Karaites of Feodosiya, lithograph (1837) by Denis-Auguste Raffet.

In their new home they adopted Turkic speech and on that basis eventually developed a distinct literary language (written in Hebrew script) that was similar to Crimean Tatar.

Hence the Karaites, like the Krymchaks, were Turkic-speaking. They differ from the rabbinite Jewish Krymchaks, however, in that the Karaites reject the religious commentaries and additions contained in authoritative compilation of Jewish law, the Talmud, and instead believe only in the word of God as given in the Hebrew Bible (Old Testament) as the sole and direct source of religious authority.

The Karaites originally settled in the port of Caffa/Kefe and beyond the coastal mountains in Solkhat/Staryi Krym, but after the fall of the Christian Principality of Theodoro-Mangup to the Ottoman Turks in 1475, they, like the Krymchaks, concentrated in the mountain-top towns of Mangup and Chufut Kale. In the eighteenth century Chufut Kale evolved into a major Karaite cultural center where, at the first publishing house anywhere in Crimea (1734), several books were printed in Hebrew and in the distinct Karaite Turkic literary language, which used the Hebrew, later Cyrillic, and even Roman (in Polish transcription) alphabets. In the second half of the nineteenth century, Chufut Kale was abandoned and Yevpatoriya became the major center of Karaites.

Already within the Crimean Khanate the Karaites were granted the status of a protected minority, although in the course of the eighteenth century their relations with the Ottoman authorities worsened. Their situation took a turn for the better with the onset of Russian rule in the 1780s. Eventually, the tsarist government made a legal distinction between Karaites and "other" Jews (Krymchaks and Ashkenazim). The Karaites themselves welcomed these distinctions, arguing that in contrast to Jews they were an especially honest and industrious people loyal to the tsar. Consequently, the Karaites became a privileged and often wealthy group (numbering 5,400 in Crimea in 1897) who were exempt from military service and granted religious autonomy. The most eminent Karaite scholar and writer was Abraham Firkovich from Lutsk in western Ukraine (the other historic center of Karaites), who from 1832 until his death in 1874 served the Crimean community both in Chufut Kale and in Yevpatoriya. Following Ukraine's independence, international funding agencies have during the last two decades helped to restore the historic Karaite district in Yevpatoriya, with its handsome nineteenth-century large and small kenesa (worship hall), which in 2005 was rededicated in conjunction with first worldwide Karaite cultural festival.

Karaite distinctiveness took a strange turn during World War II and the accompanying Holocaust, when Nazi Germany occupied Crimea. Already in 1935, the Nazi authorities in Berlin determined that, according to their ideological hierarchy of races, the Karaites were non-Jewish. Therefore, in contrast to the Jewish Krymchaks and Ashkenazim, who were virtually all murdered by the Nazis, Crimea's Karaites were left alone. Karaite behavior during the Holocaust ranged from indifference to the fate of Crimea's Krymchak and Ashkenazic Jews to collaboration with the Nazi administration and service in the German Army.

Chapter 8

Crimea during World War II

On 1 September 1939, Nazi Germany under the leadership of Adolf Hitler launched an all out invasion (*Blitzkreig*) against Poland. Two days later Poland's allies, Great Britain and France, declared war on Germany. World War II had begun.

The British and French declarations had little impact on German military operations in Poland. Moreover, Nazi Germany could remain confident of victory, because it had a new-found ally in its former arch-enemy, the Soviet Union. Having just concluded a non-aggression treaty (the Molotov-Ribbentrop Pact of August 1939), Hitler and Stalin cooperated in the destruction of Poland, whose territory was within a few weeks divided between Nazi Germany and the Soviet Union.

It was the second phase of World War II, however, that was to have a direct impact on Crimea. That phase began on 22 June 1941, when Hitler violated his country's treaty with Stalin and launched a full-scale invasion of the Soviet Union. Soviet forces suffered repeated defeats, so that within four months—by November 1941—German armies reached Leningrad and the outskirts of Moscow and conquered all of Soviet Belarus, Soviet Ukraine, and subsequently territory eastward as far as Stalingrad on the lower Volga River and southward to the foothills of the Caucasus Mountains.

As part of its military thrust into southern Ukraine, German forces under General Erich von Manstein, together with a small number of Romanian allied troops, arrived at the isthmus of Perekop in the last week of September 1941. Soviet forces put up a strong defence, but within a month they were in retreat and most of the peninsula was in German hands. The greatest challenge faced by the German invaders was the area around the Black Sea port of Sevastopol, where under the capable leadership of General Ivan Petrov Soviet soldiers were able to defend the city for nearly eight months. Only after seemingly unending battles and heavy casualties, including repeated clashes on the same hills near Balaklava of nineteenth-century Crimean War fame, did the

◀ Remember, *part one (1998) of a cycle of paintings by the Crimean Tatar artist Rustem Eminov depicting the May 1944 deportation his people.*

Germans finally succeed in capturing the largely destroyed city of Sevastopol in early July 1942.

As the Soviet military and civil authorities were being pushed out of Crimea in October and early November 1941, they hoped to leave little of strategic value to the German troops. Therefore, Soviet administrators were ordered to blow up all industrial plants that could not otherwise be removed, as well as to destroy warehouses with foodstuffs, water and sewage facilities, and electrical and telephone lines. Such deliberate destruction rendered life ex-

German soldiers on the streets of Feodosiya.

tremely difficult for Crimea's inhabitants during the winter of 1941-1942. As in other places which were about to fall to the Germans, the retreating Soviet security forces (NKVD) murdered a large number of inmates in prisons, in particular political prisoners held in Simferopol of Crimean Tatar and other ethnic backgrounds.

On the eve of the German invasion, Hitler and his advisors contemplated dividing the defeated Soviet Union into seven regions, one of which was designated "Ukraine and the Crimea." Nazi Germany was successful in subduing only the western regions of the Soviet Union, where one of the administrative units it created was the Reichskommissariat Ukraine (formed on 20 August 1941). This was essentially a German foreign colony ruled by a Nazi civil administrator (*Reichskommissar* Erich Koch) resident in the Volhynian town of Rivne.

Crimea, which was technically a part of the Reichskommissariat Ukraine, was of particular interest to Nazi Germany. Not only did it have strategic military value (control of Crimea protected Germany's southern flank and access to Ukraine), it was also an important component of Nazi ideology. Hitler decided that Crimea, after resettlement by ethnic Germans from southern Tyrol and Romania, would be transformed into a pure German colony called Gotenland (the Land of Goths), whose main cities, Simferopol and Sevastopol, would henceforth be known respectively as Gotenberg and Theodorichhafen. As

*Edige Kirimli (1911-1980)
returning from exile to
German-controlled Crimea.*

part of Hitler's "Gotenland Project," the German military undertook archeological expeditions in the coastal towns of Alushta, Gurzuf, and Inkerman (whose fortifications were presumed to be typical examples of medieval German architecture), but most importantly at the mountain-top fortress remains of Mangup, the alleged center (Doros) of the kingdom of Crimean Goths in the third and fourth centuries CE.

According to Hitler's plans for German cultural reclamation, the peninsula's Slavic inhabitants (Russians and Ukrainians) and its Crimean Tatars would have to be removed. All these peoples were dispensable, since according to Nazi racial theories they were sub-humans (*Untermenschen*), who should not be allowed to live in Crimea—a land once home to what was described as the civilized Kingdom of Goths that now could finally be recovered for the pristine German race.

Nazi policy had to be adjusted, how-

ever, to practical politics. Since Germany was anxious to have Turkey (which remained neutral for most of the war) as an active military ally, it felt obliged to tone down its racial rhetoric and, in the words of one historian of the period, "to handle the Crimean Tatar question delicately."[1] As head of the German military command, General Manstein in particular was sympathetic to some kind of accommodation with the Crimean Tatars, who were thought to be more reliable than the local Slavic population. Remembering the horrors of de-kulakization, forced collectivization, political purges, and other excesses of Stalinist rule, it is not surprising that certain elements among the Crimean Tatars might see the Germans as liberators from Soviet rule.

Putting aside Nazi racial ideology, the German military in Crimea, in cooperation with Crimean Tatar leaders who returned from exile in Turkey (Jafar Seydamet and Edige Kirimli) and Romania (Mustejip Ülküsal), organized the release of Soviet Army soldiers of Crimean Tatar background. They represented only a portion of the estimated 90,000 Soviet soldiers captured in Crimea, all of whom faced a lingering death in German prisoner-of-war camps. The Crimean Tatars who served directly or indirectly in the German war effort can be grouped into three categories.

The first came into being already in late 1941, when the Germans allowed the formation of self-defense police units and brigades comprised of about 6,000 Crimean Tatar volunteers based in

Crimean mysticism

When during World War II the Germans occupied Crimea, they organized archeological excavations in an effort to uncover remnants of what they considered the peninsula's once great Gothic civilization. This activity was carried out in secrecy by a Nazi German institution known as the Ahnenerbe, the Society for German Ancestral Heritage, which was co-founded and was under the protection of the head of the SS, Heinrich Himmler. Archeologists and anthropologists in SS uniforms carried out some excavations around the mountain-top "cave towns" of Mangup and Chufut-Kale. They also undertook some anthropological measurements among Crimean Tatars, in the hope of finding those with "Aryan blood." Should Nazi Germany win the war, these lucky "Aryans" would survive and perhaps even be favored in the new Crimea—renamed Gotenland.

Nazi mystics viewed Crimea as a possible location of what Christian Europe had been seeking since the Middle Ages—the Holy Grail, the chalice from which Jesus Christ drank at the last supper or in which his blood was collected after his crucifixion. Such hopes were encouraged by the fact that the coat-of-arms of the Principality of Mangup-Theodoro, also known as the Principality of Gothia, carried the image of a cradle which seemed to look like a cup. Hitler already had in his possession the spear of the Roman centurion Longin (who mercifully quickened the death of the crucified Christ by penetrating his chest), which the Führer had confiscated from the Habsburg imperial treasury after Nazi Germany annexed Austria. Hitler believed that Longin's spear would give him power over the whole world, provided that he could find the Holy Grail. Consequently, as the war was raging throughout Europe, Nazi Germany continued as before to dispatch specialists to the far ends of the earth, from Tibet to Antarctica, in search of the Holy Grail. One possible location for this heretofore inaccessible treasure was Crimea, the mysterious land of the ancient Goths.

Even earlier, in 1927, an expedition with a similar goal (although without the racial component) was arranged by the Soviet secret police (NKVD). It was headed by Aleksandr Barchenko, a medical doctor and scientist of Ukrainian background, whose reputation as a seer was enhanced when he predicted the disastrous earthquake that shook Crimea the same year. It was during Barchenko's rummaging among the stones of Mangup that his interest in the "occult sciences" led him to make contact with a mystical Muslim religious fraternity, the so-called whirling dervishes, who had also at the time found followers among the Crimean Tatars.

The Soviet occultists were less fortunate than their German mystical colleagues. This is because the priest-like guardians of Marxism-Leninism would not tolerate any ideological competition. Aside from Barchenko, there were other romantic enthusiasts of the Bolshevik Revolution who dreamed of creating for the Communist future a new and harmoniously balanced human, made possible by unlocking the secrets of ancient civilizations. Stalin, however, preferred the system of Gulag prisons and the spread of fear as much more effective means to control society than some ancient symbols. To be sure, for a sober-minded tyrant *like Stalin an army of obedient slaves was certainly more reliable—and pliable—than super-humans, inspired by ancient myths. Therefore, Barchenko's occultist speculations were dismissed. He and his colleagues were accused of belonging to an anti-Soviet Masonic lodge and shot by the Soviet security service (NKVD) at the end of 1930s.*

Nevertheless, dreamers of all ages continue to set out for Crimea in order to climb the mountain-top site of Mangup and other mystical places in search of possible traces of the Goths, the Holy Grail, or whatever other treasures they believe might give them supernatural powers. In the past, such mystical searches in Crimea cost some adventurers their lives. At the present, the costs to individuals consist of spent human energy and unfulfilled hopes, often accompanied by amateurish destruction of archeological remains and historic sites.

Nadiya Kushko

over 200 villages.[2] The second category included former Soviet soldiers released from German prisoner-of-war camps. About 8,700 of them were Crimean Tatars, who by early 1942 had joined the ranks of the German Army (Wehrmacht) serving on various fronts until the end of the war. The third category consisted of 1,600 volunteers, who were organized into eight (later ten) battalions under the direction of the SS and German police in Crimea. The primary purpose of the battalions was to protect German administrative and military installations at key urban centers throughout the peninsula and to fight against Soviet partisans and all real or suspected anti-Nazi elements. Despite the fact that these formations were popularly known as "Crimean Tatar battalions," their ranks included as many Russians and other nationalities as Crimean Tatars, all under the command of former Soviet officers mostly of non-Tatar origin.

As part of its policy of accommodation, the German civil authority through the representative of the Reichskommissariat in Crimea Alfred Frauenfeld, permitted already in November 1941 the formation of a Muslim Committee based in Simferopol with branches throughout the peninsula. The primary function of the Muslim Committee and its branches was to promote Crimean Tatar religious and cultural activity, including the reestablishment in Simferopol of the Crimean National Theater (closed by the Soviets in 1930s) and the publication of a Crimean Tatar language newspaper, *Azat Kirim* (Free

*Crimean Tatar soldiers
serving in the Wehrmacht led
by a German officer.*

Crimea, 1942-44). The former exile from Turkey, Edige Kirimli, who was recognized by the German authorities as the leading spokesperson for Crimean Tatar interests, even expected that some form of autonomy would be accorded his people. Such an eventuality was never part of Nazi Germany's long-term plans for Crimea. Nevertheless, in the interim, the Germans did try to cooperate with whatever elements it could, at least until the war was over. In that regard, the Crimean Tatars were not the only part of the population granted minimal favors from the occupying regime. For instance, the official languages in use were actually German and Russian, and several Russians held posts in local town and city administrations.

In contrast to the somewhat accommodating policies of the military and civil authorities, there was also the German administration responsible for the SS (units of the elite Nazi para-military organization that included the "Crimean

Tatar battalions"), the special extermination task forces (*Einsatzgruppen*) of the Security Service (SD), and the local police. The main goal of these forces was to eliminate all elements opposed to the Nazi German order, in particular Soviet partisan groups as well as the peninsula's Jewish population, both the indigenous Turkish-speaking Krymchaks (but not Karaites) as well as urban and rural Ashkenazi dwellers who had not managed to flee eastward with the retreating Soviet administration before November 1941. All in all, the German authorities deported from Crimea 85,000 mostly Russians as forced laborers (*Ostarbeiter*), while the *Einsatzgruppen* and SS units killed outright another 130,000 inhabitants (Slavs as well as Tatars in over 100 villages burned down by Wehrmacht punitive units), of whom 30,000 to 40,000 were Krymchak and Ashkenazi Jews liquidated already before the summer of 1942.[3]

Regardless of Nazi Germany's conflicting policies toward Crimean Tatars, many remained loyal to the Soviet fatherland. An estimated 20,000 fought on various fronts in the ranks of the Soviet Army, where thousands were given medals for bravery, including eight who were awarded the highest honor, Hero of the Soviet Union. Meanwhile, at home in Crimea, some Tatars had formed their own anti-German partisan groups as early as 1941-1942, although initially very few joined Soviet partisan units. This is likely because of the attacks by Soviet partisans against several Tatar-inhabited villages, which reflected the belief of Crimea's Soviet partisan commander, Aleksei V. Mokrousov, that "the vast majority of the Crimean Tatars living in mountains and foothills have gone over to the fascists."[4]

Only after the advance of the Soviet armies did Crimean Tatars (including deserters from the peninsula's various German units) begin to join Soviet partisan ranks. Their overall numbers remained small: at the outset of 1944 there were only 598, a figure which nonetheless represented nearly 17 percent of the Soviet partisans fighting against the German occupation authorities, mostly in Crimea's mountainous regions.[5] Figures in this struggle, such as Izzet Khairullaev, Refat Mustafaev, Mustafa Selimov, Bekir Osmanov have—if only recently—been resurrected as legendary Tatar heroes of Crimea's anti-German Soviet partisan movement. At the same time, a certain percentage of Crimean Tatars cooperated actively or passively with the occupying Nazi regime. Such cooperation provoked antagonism and deep hatred on the part of the local Slavic inhabitants (Russians and Ukrainians), who more often than not considered all their Crimean Tatar neighbors to be collaborators. The collaborationist label was to remain and to have dire consequences once the Soviet regime returned to power.

The turning point for the Soviet Union in World War II was the surrender of the German Army at Stalingrad in January 1943. From then on Soviet forces moved steadily westward, so that by November they were in control of all southern Ukraine as far as Perekop. At this point Hitler called on his generals to defend at all costs Crimea—"our second Stalingrad." The Soviet military acted cautiously, taking four months to prepare for an assault which finally began in early April 1944 from two directions—from the Perekop isthmus in the north, and from the Straits of Kerch in the east. Before the end of the month, the Germans were pushed out of the entire peninsula toward its southwestern corner, where they made their last stand at Sevastopol. Finally, on 12 May 1944, Sevastopol fell to victorious Soviet forces, so that all of Crimea was "liberated."

ПРИКАЗ
Все евреи города Феодосии и окрестностей обязаны явиться ____ 1. декабря 1941 г. от 8 час. до 12 часов дня на Сенную площадь № 3 (Базарная улица № 3) для переселения. Каждый еврей может иметь с собой исключительно носильные вещи и пищу на 2 дня. Все остальные вещи должны быть оставлены в полной сохранности в квартирах. Неисполнение приказа карается смертной казнью.

Начальник немецкой полиции безопасности С. Н. Ю. Б.

Russian-language poster (December 1941) of the Nazi German administration demanding that the Jews of Feodosiya and surrounding areas gather for "resettlement"—all were shot.

Crimean partisan unit on the day Simferopol was liberated,
13 April 1944.

Liberation had a particular meaning for the Soviet Union's wartime leader, Joseph Stalin. He was convinced that certain peoples within the Soviet sphere were untrustworthy, as was evident by their alleged collaboration with the Nazi German "fascists" who had wrought four years of brutal destruction on much of Soviet society. Therefore, the country's treacherous collaborationist peoples must be deported from their centuries-old homelands and resettled in the far distant regions of Siberia and Soviet Central Asia.

Within one week of having driven the Germans out of Crimea, on 18 May 1944, Soviet security forces (NKVD) carried out Stalin's order and began to deport the entire Crimean Tatar population. The Tatars were accused en masse of having "betrayed the [Soviet] Motherland during the Great Patriotic War" and of having "actively collaborated with the German occupying powers." As collective punishment, they were "to be exiled from the territory of the

Crimea and settled permanently . . . in the Uzbek SSR." [6]

Akhmetkhan Sultan (1920-1970), legendary Soviet Air Force pilot of Crimean Tatar background, twice awarded Hero of the Soviet Union.

116

Deportation began on what Crimean Tatars still remember as the *Qara Kün* (The Black Day)—18 May—when the inhabitants were given one hour to leave their homes at gunpoint. Remarkably, the process was completed in less than three days, by which time 183,200 Crimean Tatars were deported.[7] In a brutal fashion so characteristic of the Soviet regime under Stalin, the deportees were forced onto railway box cars for a trek of several weeks with little food or water. Hundreds died along the way, while upwards of 30,000 perished during the first year and a half after arriving at their destinations, where in many cases they were simply dumped without any shelter against the blistering summer heat of the Central Asian desert. By far the majority of deported Crimean Tatars (151,000) were resettled in the Uzbek SSR, while most of the remainder were sent to the Udmurt and Mari oblasts of the Russian SFSR.

Soviet Communist party authorities in Moscow made it clear that their goal was "to create a new Crimea according to Russian order."[8] All Crimean Tatar towns and villages were given new Russian names, and Muslim cemeteries and religious buildings were destroyed or transformed into a secular use. Within a few weeks of the massive May 1944 deportation of Crimean Tatars, Stalin issued a new order (2 June) that applied to three other of Crimea's numerically smaller peoples, all of whom—with little real evidence—were also accused of "collaboration with the fascists."

Already on the eve of the German invasion of Crimea, the peninsula's German inhabitants numbering 61,000 had been deported (August 1941) to the Subcaucasian region near Stavropol. Now, in June 1944, it was the turn of Crimea's Armenians (9,800), Bulgarians (12,600), and Greeks (16,000) who were resettled in Kazakhstan and Bashkiria. Particu-

Soviet sailors guarding the arrival of tanks at the beachhead near Kerch in eastern Crimea, April 1944.

Nazi Germany's allies: prisoners-of-war captured from the Romanian Army.

Подлежит возврату в Секретариат ГОКО (III часть)

Сов.секретно

ГОСУДАРСТВЕННЫЙ КОМИТЕТ ОБОРОНЫ

ПОСТАНОВЛЕНИЕ ГОКО № 5859сс

от 11 мая 1944 года   Москва, Кремль

О крымских татарах

В период Отечественной войны многие крымские
татары изменили Родине, дезертировали из частей
Красной Армии, обороняющих Крым и переходили на
сторону противника, вступали в сформированные нем-
цами добровольческие татарские воинские части, бо-
ровшиеся против Красной Армии; в период оккупации
Крыма немецко-фашистскими войсками, участвуя в
немецких карательных отрядах, крымские татары осо-
бенно отличались своими зверскими расправами по
отношению советских партизан, а также помогали не-
мецким оккупантам в деле организации насильствен-
ного угона советских граждан в германское рабство
и массового истребления советских людей.

Крымские татары активно сотрудничали с немец-
кими оккупационными властями, участвуя в организо-
ванных немецкой разведкой, так называемых "татар-
ских национальных комитетах" и широко использовались

- 6 -

6. Обязать НКО (т.Хрулева) передать в течение
мая-июня с.г. для усиления автотранспорта войск НКВД,
размещенных гарнизонами в районах расселения спецпе-
реселенцев - в Узбекской ССР, Казахской ССР и Кирги-
ской ССР, автомашин "Виллис" 100 штук и грузовых
250 штук, вышедших из ремонта.

7. Обязать Главнефтеснаб (т.Широкова) выделить
и отгрузить до 20 мая 1944 года в пункты по указанию
НКВД СССР автобензина 400 тонн и в распоряжение СНК
Узбекской ССР - 200 тонн.
Поставку автобензина произвести за счет равно-
мерного сокращения поставок всем остальным потреби-
телям.

8. Обязать Главснаблес при СНК СССР (т.Лопухова)
за счет любых ресурсов поставить НКПС"у 75.000 ваго-
нных досок по 2,75 мтр. каждая с поставкой их до 15 мая
с.г.; перевозку досок НКПС"у произвести своими сред-
ствами.

9. Наркомфину СССР (т.Звереву) отпустить НКВД
СССР в мае с.г. из резервного фонда СНК СССР на про-
ведение специальных мероприятий 30 миллионов рублей.

ПРЕДСЕДАТЕЛЬ ГОСУДАРСТВЕННОГО
КОМИТЕТА ОБОРОНЫ   И.СТАЛИН

Послано т.т. Молотову, Берия, Маленкову, Микояну,
Вознесенскому, Андрееву, Косыгину, Гриценко,
Доупову, Абдурахманову, Кобулову (НКВД УзССР),
Чадаеву - все; Багалину, Горкину, ?????

Смирнову, Субботину, Бенедиктову, Лобанову,
Звереву, Кагановичу, Митереву, Любимову,
Кравцову, Хрулеву, Жукову, Широкову, Лопухову -
соответственно.

First and last pages of the decree on Crimean Tatar deportation, signed 11 May 1944 by the chairman of the Soviet State Defense Committee, Joseph Stalin.

larly problematic was finding some justification for deporting the Greeks, a high percentage of whom fought in the ranks of the Soviet Army or in the Crimean Soviet partisan movement. In the end, over 288,000 persons were deported by Soviet authorities in 1944. [9] In effect, Crimea was ethnically cleansed, so that by the time of the first postwar census (1959) the vast majority of the population of 1.2 million comprised East Slavs, in particular Russians (71 percent) and Ukrainians (22 percent).

Before World War II came to a close, Crimea was thrust into the international spotlight. At the outset of 1945, when the Allied Powers were on the verge of defeating Nazi Germany, their leaders needed to discuss tactical issues concerning the remaining military campaign in Europe and, in particular, to lay out their strategy for the postwar world. President Franklin D. Roosevelt of the United States and Prime Minister Winston Churchill of Great Britain ac-

There are no known photographs of the departure of Crimean Tatars. This image, sometimes assumed to date from May 1944, actually shows the first returnees en route homeward to Crimea in the late 1960s.

cepted Marshal Joseph Stalin's invitation to meet personally on Soviet territory.

Stalin chose Crimea as the place to meet, since it afforded him the possibility to host his distinguished guests in the grand style to which he assumed they were accustomed. At a time when the Soviet Union and its inhabitants were still suffering from severe food shortages and other depredations caused by the war, and when Crimea and Yalta itself were substantially damaged, the Soviets hastily restored three nineteenth-century palaces just west of Yalta to a degree of their former glory. Stalin stayed at the Yusupov Palace in Koreyiz, Churchill was made "to feel at home" in the English Tudor Revival-style Vorontsov Palace in Alupka, while Roosevelt was given pride of place at the tsarist palace in Livadiya, which also served as the site of the Yalta Conference proceedings (4-11 February 1945). The sumptuous environment created by the Soviets undoubtedly helped Stalin gain much of what he wanted—and even more than he expected—from the negotiations, which resulted in agreements of profound importance for the future of Europe and postwar international relations worldwide.

It was the increase of Soviet military and political influence in central and eastern Europe that subsequently provoked the most controversy. Ever since Yalta, opinion in the West has been especially critical of President Roosevelt for having allegedly capitulated to Stalin. Indeed, during the next several decades marked by the Cold War, many inhabitants living in the Soviet satellite countries (East Germany, Poland, Czechoslovakia, Hungary, Romania, Bulgaria)

"The Big Three": Winston Churchill of Great Britain, Franklin D. Roosevelt of the United States, Joseph Stalin of the Soviet Union, and their closest advisors in the courtyard of the Livadiya Palace at the close of the Yalta Conference, 11 February 1945.

were convinced that their national sovereignty was sacrificed at Yalta. Therefore, while Crimea's Yalta remained a positive image in the minds of Soviet citizens as a place of rest and relaxation, elsewhere it became a negative symbol associated with the division of Europe for most of the second half of the twentieth century.

Ethnic cleansing Soviet Style

Well before the end of the twentieth century, when the term ethnic cleansing began to be used to describe the forced resettlement or annihilation of specific peoples, the Soviet Union already had much experience with such policies. One need only to paraphrase Stalin's infamous remark: net naroda, net problemy—no people, no problem. At the close of World War II, Stalin's convictions were once again put into practice when he ordered that Chechens, Meskhetian Turks, Crimean Tatars, and many smaller minorities be forcibly removed from their historic homelands.

This was the context for the forcible removal of over 188,000 Crimean Tatars, which began on what the deportees themselves and their descendents still remember as the Qara Kün/ "The Black Day"—18 May 1944. The terror unleashed that day by troops of the Soviet Security Service (NKVD) against innocent civilians was set in motion one week earlier by the Soviet State Defense Committee Decree No. 5859ss, dated 11 May 1944. Signed by Stalin himself, the decree listed various procedures related specifically to the deportation and resettlement of the Crimean Tatars. The government was expected to provide compensation for the immovable property taken from deportees. This never happened. Each family could bring 500 kilograms (1,000 pounds) of personal property. Considering the speed of the deportation, this was possible in only rare cases. Doctors, nurses, food, and water were assigned to each transport, but they were woefully inadequate. Between May 1944 and January 1946, nearly 27,000 Crimean Tatars (15 percent of the total) died on the way to, or after they had arrived in the special settlements to which they were assigned. One Russian eyewitness reported what he remembers of the deportation:

> It was a journey of lingering death in cattle railway cars, crammed with people, like mobile gas chambers. The journey lasted three to four weeks and took them across the scorching summer steppes of Kazakhstan. They took the Red partisans of Crimea, the fighters of the Bolshevik underground, and Soviet and [Communist] party activists. Also invalids and old men. The remaining men were fighting at the front, but deportation awaited them at the end of the war. And in the meantime they crammed their women and children into trucks, where they constituted the vast majority. Death mowed down the old, the young, and the weak. They died of thirst, suffocation, and the stench.
>
> On the long stages the corpses decomposed in the middle of the cattle cars, and at the short halts, where water and food were handed out, the people were not allowed to bury their dead and had to leave them beside the railway track.*

* Cited in Ann Sheehy, The Crimean Tatars and Volga Germans: Soviet Treatment of Two National Minorities. Minority Rights Group Report, No. 6 (London, 1971), pp. 10-11.

Chapter 9

Soviet Crimea and Exiled Crimean Tatars

By 8 May 1945, when World War II formally came to a close in Europe, not only had the forces of Nazi Germany and its allies been driven out of Crimea, but the peninsula had also been cleansed of most of its Crimean Tatar and other non-East Slavic inhabitants. The Soviet authorities were now able to fashion a new Crimea, seemingly without having to be concerned about any "foreign" ethnocultural burdens from the historical past. The subsequent remaking of Crimea was the result of a broad range of administrative, demographic, and socioeconomic policy changes.

Since there were no more Tatars living in Crimea, from the Soviet Union's perspective there was no need for a national republic. Hence, on 30 June 1945 the Crimean Autonomous Soviet Socialist Republic created in 1921 was abolished, and Crimea was downgraded to the status of an ordinary administrative subdivision (oblast) of the Russian Soviet Federated Socialist Republic. Aside from this administrative change, the postwar Soviet regime set out to obliterate all memory of the Tatars and

their age-old presence in Crimea. Hundreds of Crimean Tatar libraries, village reading rooms, schools, and clubs were simply destroyed and all mosques were closed.[1] That the Crimean Tatars themselves were gone was not enough, however. It was necessary to forget that they had ever been in Crimea.

The first step of this process came immediately after the 1944 deportation. In a concerted effort to change the cultural landscape, most Tatar names of towns and villages were replaced by rather bland Slavic names—first sometimes awkward Russian forms and later their Ukrainian equivalents—which either alluded to a local geographic feature or, more commonly, to some Soviet heroic personage or event. Hence, Crimean Tatar Karasubazar became Belogorsk/Bilohirsk (White Mountain), Dzhurchi—Pervomaiskoe/Pervomaiske (The First of May), Qurman—Krasnogvardeiskoe/Krasnohvardiiske (The Red Guard), Ichki—Sovetskoe/Sovetskyi (The Soviet), Islâm Terek—Kirovskoe/Kirovske (Kirov's Town), and Yedi Quyu—Lenino/Lenine (Lenin's Town).

◄ *Mustafa Jemiloglu/Dzhemilev (b. 1943), the most famous Crimean Tatar dissident and revered leader of the Crimean Tatar people.*

The next step was to expunge Crimean Tatars and the Crimean Khanate from Soviet history textbooks and reference works. Instead, Greco-Byzantine civilization, its relationship to Kievan Rus', and in particular Catherine II's conquest of 1783 and the presence of famous Russian nineteenth-century military and cultural figures in Crimea were what was considered worthy of remembering. Of particular importance in this regard was the city of Sevastopol. As home base to the Black Sea Fleet, Sevastopol was raised to mythological proportions as the *gorod-geroi* (City of Heroes) and the *gorod russkoi slavy* (City of Russian Glory); that is, the ultimate symbol of Russian and Soviet resistance during two bloody sieges, the first (lasting 349 days) during the Crimean War of 1854-1855, the second (lasting 250 days) during World War II. No expense was spared to restore the late-nineteenth panorama depicting the first siege and then to build another complex, this time a diorama to commemorate the successful assault by the Soviet Army and liberation of the city in May 1944.

As for the Crimean Tatars, they may have existed in the past, but in the words of the Communist party-sanctioned second revised edition of the *Great Soviet Encyclopedia* (1953), their "primary purpose was war and pillaging raids for plunder and profit," serving as willing tools of the Ottoman "Turks in their struggle against the Slavic peoples" north of the Black Sea.[2] Consequently, it was the Crimean Tatars who kept the region from normal development. This ideologically motivated viewpoint was made abundantly clear in a new four-volume history of the region: "The Crimean Tatars, accustomed to living on profits gained from plundering raids," had little aptitude for "productive labor," and for those reasons "Crimea remained a poor and backward region until it was ceded [in 1783] to Russia."[3]

History writing was always an instrument of Soviet state policy, and Marxist historians got their marching orders in the wake of a three-day conference of leading Soviet scholars held in Simferopol in 1952. As reported in the All-Union Communist party newspaper, *Pravda* (The Truth), the eminent Soviet specialist on medieval Kievan Rus', Boris Grekov, declared in his opening speech that "the antiquated and incorrect positions, as well as the mistaken views in the historical literature about Crimea need to be completely revised." Why? Because "Crimea has always been an object lusted after by many of Russia's enemies, with the result that bourgeois historians [and this included Crimean Tatar writers within prewar Soviet Crimea], in an effort to justify the aggressive plans of their own governments, have falsified the history of Crimea." [4] Consequently, Soviet historians should in the future always keep in mind the following: everything that was Slavic (in particular Russian), or that could be linked to the Slavic world (Kievan Rus' and its relationship to Byzantine Crimea) should be praised as good, while everything that was related to the lustful enemies of Russia—the Ottoman Empire and its Crimean Tatar vassals—should be remembered as bad.

This black-and-white Soviet approach to history also applied to Russian-Ukrainian relations. Among the few pre-Soviet events in Ukrainian history that the authorities considered to be positive was the 1654 agreement of Pereyaslav, at which Ukraine's Zaporozhian Cossacks under Hetman Bohdan Khmelnytskyi pledged their loyalty to the tsar of Muscovy. The Soviets officially described this event as the re-unification of Ukraine with Russia and, on the occasion of its 300th anniversary in 1954, launched a series of public celebratory events and publications. Also at that time the Crimean oblast was formally transferred from the Russian SFSR to the Ukrainian Soviet Socialist Republic (Soviet Ukraine). The transfer, described by Soviet writers as a "gift from Russia to Ukraine" on the occasion of the 1954 Pereyaslav celebrations, was allegedly initiated by Nikita Khrushchev, someone

close to Ukraine who at the time was First Secretary of the All-Union Communist party of the Soviet Union.[5]

For the general public, the transfer of Crimea to Soviet Ukraine generally went unnoticed. After all, the Soviet Union was never a real federation of national republics, so that for the average Soviet resident in Crimea it made little difference whether he or she inhabited an administrative entity (oblast) in Soviet Russia or in Soviet Ukraine. On the other hand, the Soviet Ukrainian republic leadership took its new territorial acquisition seriously, and as early as April 1954 it submitted to Moscow a comprehensive plan to promote the development of agriculture, urban areas, and sanatoria in its Crimean oblast. While it is true that decisions about economic

The March 9, 1954 issue of the official newspaper of the Supreme Soviet of the Soviet Union announcing the transfer of Crimea from the Russian SFSR to the Ukrainian SSR.

development were made by the central government in Moscow, funding for certain projects and their implementation (including projects in the separate federal jurisdiction of Sevastopol) were channelled through Ukrainian authorities in Kyiv before reaching Crimea.

In order for the Soviet regime to advance the economic reconstruction of Crimea, it needed to address the demographic problem; that is, to replace the large number of people eliminated during the war, whether from death in prisoner-of-war camps, execution by the occupying German authorities (including political opponents as well as Jews), and deportation to Germany (*Ostarbeiter*—workers from the east). Remarkably, two of Crimea's largest cities before the war (each with over 100,000 inhabitants) were virtually bereft of their populations, so that at the close of the conflict Sevastopol had only 1,019 inhabitants and Kerch a mere 30! These losses, combined with the deportation of Tatars and the region's other allegedly treacherous peoples (Germans, Armenians, Bulgarians, Greeks), reduced Crimea's population from 1.2 million on the eve of the war to only 351,000 by the late summer of 1944.[6]

In order to compensate for these enormous losses, systematic in-migration was fostered by the Soviet authorities. The largest number of in-migrants came from various parts of Soviet Russia (including several thousand Ashkenazi Jews who returned from evacuation zones in the east), with a lesser percentage from Soviet Ukraine. It took nearly a decade,

but by 1956 the population of Crimea had reached its prewar level of over a million. According to the first postwar census (1959), the vast majority of those inhabitants (96 percent) were East Slavs, and of those, Russians (71.4 percent) clearly predominated over Ukrainians (22.3 percent).[7] The in-migrants settled in both urban and rural areas, with the result that the Crimean peninsula was entirely slavicized. Since the Soviet regime only slowly managed to build new apartment blocks in urban areas, initially the authorities allocated to the first in-migrants property that formerly belonged to Crimean Tatars— no less than 80,000 homes, 34,000 surrounding gardens, and 500,000 head of livestock.[8] As a result, hundreds of villages and even traditional Crimean Tatar towns like Karasubazar (now Bilohirsk) and Eski Kirim (Staryi Krym) as well as districts of larger cities like Simferopol (the Aqmescit quarter) and Bakhchysaray (its old quarter) became—and to this day have remained—communities of Russian-speaking Slavs.

The postwar Soviet regime was particularly concerned with reconstructing Crimea's economy, which had been disrupted and in some sectors damaged or completely destroyed during World War II. The Soviet model of development— ever since 1928 based on a command economy directed by the All Union authorities in Moscow (Gosplan) and implemented through Five Year Plans with production goals for individual regions and enterprises—determined the direction of Crimea's economy after 1945.

Whereas industrial development was

promoted, the agricultural sector also remained an important component of the oblast's economic life. The Iron Ore Complex based in Kerch and its surrounding area, heavily damaged during the war, was not only restored but expanded, so that by 1975 it was producing 39 times as much as it had before the conflict. [9] Other enterprises that experienced expansion included the chemical plants in Armyansk (aniline and dioxide), which processed salt reserves from the Sivash Sea and inland lakes in northern Crimea, as well as various machine-building, metal-working, construction-material, plastics, and chemical industrial plants located in the oblast's largest cities: Simferopol, Sevastopol (each with over 300,000 inhabitants by the 1980s), and Kerch. Among the newer and more successful industrial enterprises was the Simferopol plant opened in the 1960s to manufacture televisions under the well-known Soviet labels, Krym and Foton, and the Zaliv Shipbuilding Plant in Kerch, which during the Soviet Union's Ninth Five-Year Plan (1971-1975) began to launch its first supertankers.

In order to provide power for these expanding industries, several regional thermoelectric stations were opened in the 1960s, drawing their energy from newly developed natural gas fields in western and northern Crimea. A milestone in socioeconomic development was reached in the mid-1960s, when electricity was brought to all towns and villages throughout Crimea.

The largest component of Crimea's economic output remained, as before, food processing, which accounted for 44 percent of all industrial production. Within that category wine remained, as before, the oblast's most lucrative product, in particular the world famous vintage dessert wines under the Massandra and Zolota Balka labels, and the extremely popular Crimean "champagne," which seemed to be found in every restaurant and household during the last decades of the Soviet Union's existence. To assure the continual flow of wines, the amount of land set aside in Crimea to cultivate grapes increased seven-fold between the 1940s and 1979.

With regard to other agricultural crops, the cultivation of cotton, greatly expanded in the 1930s, was completely abandoned, while the tobacco industry, especially higher quality blends such as the Dyubek brand, were encouraged to expand. Because of its sub-tropical climate, especially along the coast and the southern slopes of the mountains, Crimea continued to be a major producer of fruits, nuts, and essencial oil plants (rose, lavender, rosemary, and sage). To assure the year-long cultivation of these products as well as grains and industrial crops grown on the treeless northern steppe, the Soviet Ukrainian government in cooperation with central agencies in Moscow funded the construction of reservoirs, and between 1963 and 1975 completed the North Crimean Canal. It stretched from the lower Dnieper River through the Perekop isthmus, continued eastward the entire length of the peninsula almost as far as Kerch, and was crossed by two branch canals that nearly reached the Black Sea just north of Yevpatoriya (see Map 1).

Crimea's mild climate also allowed for the further development of the tourist and health-resort economic sectors. In particular after Crimea became part of Soviet Ukraine, the authorities were anxious to assure the ongoing success of this profitable economic sector. The number of health-related facilities was doubled, so that by the early 1970s there were no less than 105 sanatoria and 24 rest homes which were able to accommodate 46,000 patients, as well as large state-run, industrial-scale hotel residences that could accommodate the increasingly large number of Soviet vacationers, averaging at any one time 80,000 visitors in the summer months and 45,000 in the winter.[10]

In the course of any given year as many as four million people would make use of Crimea's resorts and health facilities. To handle this enormous volume of human traffic, attractive new railway stations were built in Simferopol, Kerch, and Yevpatoriya, and in the 1970s the airport in Simferopol was expanded to accommodate the increasing number of air passengers made possible by relatively inexpensive tickets offered by state-owned airlines. The Soviet Ukrainian authorities were particularly proud of the results of their investment in the Soviet Union's first mountain trolley-bus line completed in 1961, which allowed direct access from the oblast's main rail and air arrival point, Simferopol, across the mountains to the main coastal resort centers via Alushta to Yalta.

Nor was Crimea a destination only for the Soviet Union's working masses. In effect, nothing much had changed. As in tsarist times, so too under Soviet rule the state's political elite (*nomenklatura*) flocked to Crimea to live in high style in resort areas reserved exclusively for them. Postwar Soviet leaders each

All-Union Soviet leader Nikita Khrushchev and the head of Soviet Ukraine Petro Shelest inaugurate in 1963 the first stage of the North Crimean Canal.

Crimea's mountain trolley bus line, 1960s.

had his favorite Crimean resort: for Stalin it was Koreyiz; for Brezhnev, Oreanda; and for Gorbachev, Foros.

Crimea, therefore, became a home away from home for the Soviet people. Despite the fact that Crimea was administratively part of Soviet Ukraine, and that a significant portion of its inhabitants registered themselves as Ukrainian (although more often than not they were Russian-language speakers), Crimea was culturally a Russian land, where every resident or visitor from elsewhere in the Soviet Union felt equally at home.

But what about the Tatars, who for centuries had defined the cultural landscape of Crimea? They may have been in exile thousands of kilometers away in Central Asia, but they did not go away. And they would not go away until they would be allowed to return to the homeland from which they were so brutally torn on that Black Day of 18 May 1944.

The vast majority (151,000) of the 195,000 exiled Crimean Tatars were settled in Soviet Uzbekistan. Initially, their situation bordered on the disastrous. Between May 1944 and January 1946, nearly 27,000 died as a result of unhygienic conditions, lack of clean water, overcrowding, and an outbreak of typhus on their way to, or after they arrived in, the special settlements (*spetsposelenie*) to which they were assigned. [11] The special settlements were camps surrounded by barbed wire and headed by a comman-

dant from the Soviet Ministry of Interior to whom heads of Tatar households had to report every three days. Residents were forbidden to leave the special settlement areas on pain of arrest and sentence of five years of hard labor. The exiled Tatars were denied the right to move about freely, even within the Soviet republic in which they resided, and they were explicitly banned from returning to Crimea.

Upon their arrival, most Crimean Tatars were housed in stables, sheds, and underground dug-outs, which provided minimal shelter from the extreme heat, malarial fevers, and insufficiently clean water that characterized the Central Asian steppe. Eventually, they built homes and adapted their agricultural and pastoral skills to the local environment. Their numbers also gradually increased, although not likely reaching one million as some Crimean Tatar sources reported in the 1980s. It was difficult to know the exact figures, because the Crimean Tatar designation as a distinct nationality was itself abolished by a Soviet decree in

ЛЕНИН БАЙРАГЪЫ

Яшасын I Майыс куни—эмекдарларнынъ халкъара бирдемлик ве бутюн мемлекетлер ишчилеринынъ къардашлыкъ куни!

Ленинизмнынъ гъалибиети

Lenin Bayragi *(The Flag of Lenin),* *newspaper for Crimean Tatars* *in exile published in Tashkent,* *the capital of Soviet Uzbekistan.*

1946, after which they were subsumed under the general rubric *Tatar,* which referred to Volga Tatars, Siberian Tatars, and Tatars in other Soviet republics, as well as Crimean Tatars.

After the death of Stalin in 1953, the legal status of the Crimean Tatar exiles gradually improved. Between 1954 and 1956, the restrictions on movement were lifted, but they were still not able to acquire fields in the few irrigated areas of Uzbekistan, where arable land was at a premium. Consequently, many migrated to the republic's small towns and cities, in particular its capital Tashkent. This meant that people who had traditionally made their livelihood as agriculturalists or pastoralists in the Crimean homeland now worked in mines and factories, usually at jobs not wanted by local Uzbeks. This was particularly the case among Crimean Tatar males and females born in and/or largely raised in exile.

In 1957, the Soviet central government in Moscow issued a decree concerning several of the nationalities it had deported in 1944 and absolved them of the charge of treason. The Crimean

Tatars were not, however, on the list of those absolved. On the other hand, that same year did see the appearance in Tashkent of a newspaper in the Crimean Tatar language, *Lenin Bayragi* (The Flag of Lenin). During the next decade, other Crimean Tatar institutions came into being in the capital of Soviet Uzbekistan: a literary council, publishing house, language and literature department at the pedagogical institute, and in the 1980s a literary journal *Yildiz* (The Star). Such cultural and educational developments together with greater freedom of movement (at least within the republics of their exile) helped motivate younger Crimean Tatars to meet in informal gatherings, which before long formulated two clear goals: national rehabilitation and the right to return to Crimea.

The first phase of Crimean Tatar organizational activity took the form of petitions submitted to the Soviet authorities. The first of these, sent to the Supreme Soviet in June 1957, included 6,000 signatures. Several other petitions followed, culminating in one delivered in October 1961 to the 21st Party Congress of the All-Union Communist party with over 25,000 signatures. Invoking "Leninist nationality policies," all of the petitions repeated the same demands: national rehabilitation and the right to return to Crimea. The immediate response of the Soviet authorities was to arrest Crimean Tatar activists in Uzbekistan on the grounds that they were producing and distributing "anti-Soviet propaganda" and "stirring up racial discord." [12]

The arrests did not intimidate but rather galvanized what was becoming a Crimean Tatar national movement. Its next stage, between 1962 and 1966, witnessed the creation of committees in each exile community, whose goal was to tell Crimean Tatars the truth about their historical past distorted by Soviet writers and about the injustice of their deportation. Among these grass-roots committees was the Union of Crimean Youth, co-founded by Mustafa Jemiloglu/Dzhemilev, soon to become the most renowned Crimean Tatar dissident. The committees in exile began to send delegations to Moscow to deliver even more petitions. One of these, a petition addressed to the 23rd All-Union Communist party congress, was signed by no less than 120,000 persons, virtually the entire adult Crimean Tatar population in exile. Finally, in July 1967, a group of Crimean Tatars managed to gain an audience in the Kremlin with several high-ranking Soviet officials, including the head of the state security services (KGB), Yuri Andropov. Several promises were made, one of which was realized a few months later (September 1967), when a Soviet decree annulled the 1944 "decision of state organs which contained indiscriminate accusations with respect to citizens of Tatar nationality who lived in Crimea." [13] Whereas Crimean Tatars as a group may have been absolved of wartime treason, this decree of limited

The first spontaneous Crimean Tatar demonstration in the Soviet Union's capital Moscow (1987) that was not dispersed by the authorities.

rehabilitation said nothing about compensation for the victims of the state's policies or of any right of return to the Crimean homeland.

The Crimean Tatar exiles nevertheless persisted in what now became a concerted campaign for the right to return. In the absence of any formal permission, in 1967 and 1968 upwards of 10,000 Tatars simply left Uzbekistan and returned to Crimea. Local officials, who were incensed by such boldness, invoked the only weapon they had: refusal to grant them a *propiska*; that is, to register them as residents, which according to Soviet law was a necessary pre-condition for anyone seeking employment and accommodation. Attempts to set up tents as temporary shelter were squashed with force by the KGB and local police who deported all the "illegals" back to Uzbekistan. In the end, only about 900 Tatar families managed to secure permanent settlement in Crimea in 1968-1969, although their fate remained precarious. For the next two decades the returnees were frequently harassed by the authorities. In desperation, a few Crimean Tatars chose to protest their unenviable situation by public self-immolation, the most famous example being Musa Mamut, who perished in 1978 after pouring gasoline over his body and setting himself on fire.

Nevertheless, the right-to-return campaign continued among the exiles in Uzbekistan, where Crimean Tatar activists formulated petitions to the central Soviet authorities and organized public demonstrations. The Soviet regime believed it could crush the movement by arresting the leading Crimean Tatar ac-

Musa Mamut (1931-1978), photographed before his death by sel-fimmolation.

Refat Chubarov (b. 1957), present chairman of the Mejlis, kneeling (second from the left) before the burial place of the martyr Musa Mamut.

tivists. Beginning in 1969, major trials were held in Tashkent for three consecutive years in a row, and several activists, including decorated Red Army veterans of World War II (the Great Fatherland War in Soviet terminology), were sentenced to various terms in prison. The trials not only failed to eliminate the Crimean Tatar movement, but managed to attract the attention of supporters who were part of the more general democratic and human-rights movement in the Soviet Union. Among the dissidents who linked their own fate directly with the Crimean Tatar cause was a Jewish activist from Baku, Ilya Gabai, and the retired Red Army Major General of Ukrainian origin, Petro Hryhorenko/Petr Grigorenko. Particularly outspoken was Hryhorenko, who on the eve of the 1969 Tashkent trial spoke of "two accursed Führers of the twentieth century," one of whom was the "Marxist" Stalin who carried out genocide against the Crimean Tatars.[14] Finally, it was solidarity on the part of high-profile Soviet dissidents, like Andrei Sakharov and his wife Elena Bonner (both present at the 1976 Omsk trial of Mustafa Dzhemilev), that brought the Crimean Tatar problem to the attention of the Western media.

It was not until the second half of the 1980s, however, that the status of the Crimean Tatars was transformed in any significant way. This was related to a change in leadership in the Soviet Union, which in March 1985 saw the accession of Mikhail Gorbachev to the post of secretary general of the Communist party, the most powerful position in the Soviet Union. Gorbachev set out to reform the ailing economy of the country through what was called restructuring (*perestroika*) and openness (*glasnost*); that is, by doing away with the centralized command economy and encouraging the democratic-like participation of all citizens in the transformation of Soviet society. Gorbachev's efforts at reform led to a loosening of control over many aspects of society by the central government and its security apparatus, to the eventual end of the Communist party's monopolization on power, and to a general liberalization and removal of legal restrictions imposed by Stalin and his successors.

Symbolic of the new political environment was the response to a Crimean Tatar demonstration that took place in July 1987 in Red Square, the symbolic center of Soviet power. Instead of responding with force and arrests, the authorities established a commission to consider Crimean Tatar demands. Two years later the Supreme Soviet (parliament) of the Soviet Union issued a decree (November 1989), which recognized the right of the Crimean Tatars to return. That decision sparked a surge of migration: if in 1989 there were only about 20,000 Tatars in Crimea, by June 1991 their number had reached 135,000.[15]

Gorbachev's reformist policies also touched off a debate about the future of Crimea within the rapidly changing Soviet Union. Like other peripheral regions of the Soviet Union, Crimea had been slow to accept Gorbachev's call for restructuring and openness. The local Communist authorities, whose policies reflected the region's close relationship with the highest echelons of the older Soviet ruling elite (*nomenklatura*) which regularly vacationed and often retired in Crimea, were known for their reactionary conservatism and unquestioning conformity to policies set in Moscow. By 1989, however, there were increasing discussions about the desirability of restoring Crimea to its pre-World War II status as an autonomous soviet socialist republic—ASSR. The local communist elites saw autonomy as a convenient means to enrich themselves through the mechanism of a Free Economic Zone, as well as an instrument by which they might be able to deter, or at least limit, the return of Tatars to Crimea. The discussions about autonomy also led to speculation about whether a renewed Crimean autonomous republic should remain with Soviet Ukraine or be returned to Soviet Russia. In keeping with Gorbachev's

call for public participation in political decision-making, a referendum on this issue was indeed held in Crimea at the very outset of 1991. An overwhelming majority of the eligible electorate—no less than 93 percent—voted for the re-creation of the Crimean Soviet Socialist Republic within the framework of a restructured Soviet Union.[16]

Meanwhile, Soviet Ukraine, of which Crimea was still formally a part, was redefining its own relationship to the Soviet Union, and in July 1990, the Supreme Soviet (parliament) in Kyiv declared Ukraine a sovereign state. Reacting quickly to the referendum in Crimea, the parliament in Kyiv within one month (February 1991) recognized the restoration of the Crimean ASSR, but within Soviet Ukraine.

Finally, the Crimean Tatars, whose numbers continued to swell with the arrival of returnees from Central

One of many Crimean Tatar protest meetings in support of national rights, Simferopol (1990s).

Recently erected monument in Feodosiya to the victims of Bolshevik terror during the years 1918-1922.

Asia, were thrust into the rapidly changing political arena. In June 1991, delegates from all re-established Tatar communities throughout Crimea gathered in Simferopol at a national assembly (*Kurultay*) to express their views about the future of their homeland. They adopted a declaration on national sovereignty, announced their intention to re-establish a sovereign Crimean Tatar state, and created a representative organ, the Mejlis, to advocate for their political demands.

Hence, by the summer of 1991, there were three forces claiming to represent the political interests of Crimea: (1) sovereign Soviet Ukraine, of which the Crimean ASSR was legally a part; (2) the Communist-dominated Supreme Soviet (parliament) of the Crimean ASSR, many of whose members favored remaining with the Soviet Union or a future Russian state should Ukraine secede; and (3) the Mejlis, which was determined to refashion Crimea into a Tatar national republic. This was the situation in August 1991, when events in far-away Moscow set the stage for new changes that were to have a profound impact not only on Crimea but on the entire Soviet Union.

Chapter 10

Crimea in Independent Ukraine

On 21 August 1991, conservative political forces in Moscow staged a coup d'état (putsch) with the intent to overthrow Mikhail Gorbachev, who, in the tradition of Soviet leaders, was at the time on summer vacation with his family in Crimea. The coup failed, and within a few days, on 24 August, the parliament in Kyiv declared Ukraine an independent state. The declaration also called for a public referendum on independence to be held before the end of the year, on 1 December 1991, the same day as the first national elections for Ukraine's president.

Crimea's parliament in Simferopol reacted quickly to the new political situation. The parliament issued a "Declaration of Crimean State Sovereignty" (September 1991) and proclaimed itself the supreme authority in Crimea responsible for all state property. While the parliament confirmed its intention to remain within Ukraine, it also issued statements that questioned the legitimacy of the 1954 transfer of Crimea from Soviet Russia to Soviet Ukraine. Clearly, political leaders in Kyiv and Simferopol had differing views about Crimea's relationship to Ukraine.

In effect, three forces jockeyed for control of Crimea in the early 1990s: the regional parliament in Simferopol; Ukraine's central authorities in Kyiv; and the executive organ (Mejlis) of the Crimean Tatar national assembly (Kurultay). Crimea's parliament, many of whose Communist party deputies belonged to the recently established Republican Movement of Crimea headed by Yuriy Meshkov, supported a high degree of regional self-rule. Local business entrepreneurs were of the same view, while some civic activists pushed even further, calling for Crimea's return to Russia or its complete independence. Meanwhile, government and parliamentary leaders in Kyiv, in particular supporters of the Ukrainian national-democratic movement called RUKH, recognized that while Crimea should have a degree of autonomy (self-rule), ultimate authority

◄ *Chersonesus near Sevastopol. The nineteenth-century St. Vladimir Russian Orthodox Cathedral, destroyed during World War II, restored 1997-2001 under the patronage of the presidents of Ukraine (Leonid Kuchma) and Russia (Vladimir Putin).*

Crimea's Russian civilians and war veterans at a demonstration in Sevastopol (1990s) under the portraits of Lenin and Stalin

rested with the state of which it was a part—Ukraine. Finally, there were the Crimean Tatars represented by their own "parliament," the Kurultay, with its executive organ, the Mejlis. Headed by the former anti-Soviet dissident and prisoner of conscience, Mustafa Dzhemilev, the Mejlis saw itself as a proto-governmental institution prepared to lead a self-governing Crimea which should be reconstructed as a democratic republic that recognized the special role of the region's three indigenous peoples (*korennye narody*): Crimean Tatars, Krymchaks, and Karaites.

The Crimean public expressed its views on the various political options in the 1 December 1991 referendum on Ukraine's independence and presidential elections. The majority of voters favored Ukraine's independence (54 percent) and voted for the candidate, Leonid Kravchuk (57 percent), who won the elections and became the newly independent country's first president. The results suggested that Crimea's inhabitants were ambivalent about their homeland's political status and future.

For the next few years, while Ukraine's authorities were preoccupied with building governmental institutions and negotiating a constitution for its new state, Crimea followed a distinct, if somewhat erratic path. In 1992, the parliament in Simferopol adopted a first, then second constitution which called

Yuriy Meshkov (b. 1945).

into being the Republic of Crimea as a state within Ukraine. Then, in early 1994, Crimeans were urged to elect Yuriy Meshkov, the head of the pro-Russian faction (*Russkii Blok*) in parliament, as their republic's president. With the support and encouragement of politicians in Russia (among whom the most vociferous was the mayor of Moscow, Yuriy Luzhkov), Meshkov and his political allies emphasized the idea of Crimea's historic unity with Russia and the need to draw closer to that country. At the same time, the peninsula's Russian populace was constantly being reminded of the charges of World War II collaboration which allegedly lent historical justification for Stalin's 1944 wholesale deportation of the Crimean Tatars. Not surprisingly, the Crimean Tatar Mejlis was strongly opposed to the Crimean republic's pro-Russian stance. Under its ever pragmatic leader Mustafa Dzhemilev, the Mejlis based its policy on remaining within Ukraine and on cooperation with the pro-Ukrainian national-democratic RUKH forces and later with the Our Ukraine coalition.

Uncertainty about Crimea's future political status came to an end when, finally, the government in Kyiv not only adopted a clear position but also acted upon it. In 1995, Ukraine's second president, Leonid Kuchma, issue a decree which cancelled the Crimean constitution, abolished its presidency, and subordinated the Crimean government directly to Ukraine's president. Although independent Ukraine's first constitution (June 1996) provided for a centralized state, it made one exception: recognition of the Autonomous Republic of Crimea.

Ships of modern-day Russia's Black Sea Fleet anchored in the Bay of Sevastopol during the 200th anniversary celebrations in 2013 of the Russian Empire's establishment of the fleet.

*Session
of the Third
Crimean
Tatar
Kurultay in
Simferopol,
January
2001.*

In the words of Crimea's own newly-revised constitution (October 1998), it formed "an inseparable component part of Ukraine."[1] The autonomous republic's parliament in Simferopol was allotted several responsibilities, all of which were ultimately dependent on approval by Ukraine's central authorities in Kyiv. Crimea, therefore, was granted autonomy on territorial, not national principles, as the Crimean Tatars had wanted. The Crimean constitution did, however, guarantee the use in all spheres of public life of the Russian, Crimean Tatar, and other minority languages alongside the state language, Ukrainian.

Finally, there was the problem of the Black Sea port city of Sevastopol. In Soviet times, the city had a separate administrative status under the direct control of the central authorities in Moscow. Now that Ukraine was an independent state of which Crimea was a part, what should be the status of Sevastopol? Should it remain a distinct administrative entity and, if so, under the control of whose central authorities—those of Ukraine, or of Russia? In the end, the city of Sevastopol together with a good portion of the southeastern corner of Crimea—including Inkerman, Balaklava, and several inland villages—was administratively detached from the rest of the autonomous republic and placed under the direct authority of Ukraine's central government in Kyiv (see Map 1).

Further complicating the issue of Sevastopol was its function as the home port of the Black Sea Fleet. This once significant force, rebuilt by the Soviet military after World War II, was substantially reduced in size, although by the mid-1990s it still had 300 combat ships, 14 submarines, and 300 planes and helicopters staffed by over 35,000 military personnel.[2] Together with Sevastopol, the fleet was claimed by both Ukraine and Russia, causing controversy and deep friction between Moscow and Kyiv, which lasted several years until the conclusion of the Russian-Ukrainian Friendship Treaty and Black Sea Fleet Treaty (May 1997). In the end, the reduced fleet and its personnel were divided between the Russian and Ukrainian navies, while Russia was given a twenty-year lease (until 2017) to maintain its portion (80 percent) of the Black Sea Fleet in Sevastopol. In 2010, Ukraine's government under President Viktor Yanukovych extended Russia's lease for another twenty-five years (until 2042).

The political changes following the collapse of the Soviet Union in 1991 had a traumatic impact on the majority population of Crimea—its Russians. For over two centuries since 1783, ethnic Russians, whether as tsarist imperial or Soviet subjects, represented the dominant political, economic, social, and cultural force in the region. Now, Crimea's Russians found themselves in a new country, Ukraine, which, from the perspective of many, had the affrontery to designate the "uncivilized Little Russian dialect" (*malorusskoe narechie*) as the state language. And if that were not enough, Crimea's Russians were being challenged in their own "Russian" homeland by the arrival of what were looked upon as a strange people from the east—Tatars—who were claiming that Crimea was their national patrimony.

The generally worsening economic situation that characterized the post-Soviet period of transition was accompanied by several negative developments: the closure of many state-owned enterprises; an increase in unemployment; a decline in personal wealth due to rampant hyper-inflation and unpaid wages; and the precipitous rise in organized criminal gangs who arrived in Crimea from all parts of the former Soviet Union

(in particular from Chechnya). All of these factors prompted many Russians to feel that the only world they knew was collapsing beneath their feet. How could all this have happened in such a short period of time to a people who for centuries had grown accustomed to being part of a powerful and large state that traditionally ruled others? In the words of one scholar at the University of Simferopol, himself an ethnic Russian: "To ask a Russian to give up the imperial idea is like asking a Russian to cease being a Russian."[3]

The response of Crimea's Russians to their unenviable new situation has been to support the Communist party and new Russian nationalist organizations, such as the Russian Community of Crimea/Russkaya obshchina Kryma (ROK) and more recently the Crimean Cossack Union/Krymskiy kozachiy soyuz (KKS), which prefer governing in the Soviet style and which might welcome unification with Russia. These same political and civic forces hoped to deter, or at least make life difficult for returning Crimean Tatars. Others hoped to find solace in Russia's religious heritage by supporting the revival of Orthodox churches, monasteries, and the restoration of holy sites being carried out by the Moscow Patriarchate, often with the financial support of the governments of both Ukraine (especially President Leonid Kuchma) and Russia (especially Prime Minister/President Vladimir Putin).

It should, therefore, not be surprising that the return of Tatars to Crimea was not made any easier because of the conditions they encountered before and after the collapse of the Soviet Union and Ukraine's independence. The number of Tatars who began to return during the last years of Soviet rule continued unabated during the first five years of independent Ukraine to nearly 226,000. From 1997 the number of arrivals dwindled to a few thousand each year. Ukraine's official census (2001) recorded 243,000 Tatars, or 12 percent of Crimea's total population, although unofficial sources place their number at close to 300,000. Not surprisingly, the majority of returnees came from Uzbekistan (72%), followed by a significant number from southern Russia (16%), and the remainder from other former Soviet Central Asian republics.[4]

As in most places of the former Soviet Union, Crimea suffered from a severe housing shortage. This fact, combined with hostility of the local Crimean authorities who provided little or no help, forced the Tatars to live like squatters on unused state land on the outskirts of cities and towns mostly in the interior of the peninsula. For most of the 1990s, Crimea's Tatars were reduced to inhabiting ramshackle structures built out of whatever scrap material they could find, or to remain inside the very cargo containers used to transport their possessions to Crimea. Meanwhile, many local officials and residents were incensed by the presence of what they considered "foreign usurpers from the East," and it was not uncommon for the authorities to order the destruction of the shanty towns, only to see them immediately rebuilt by the determined Tatars. The fate of the returnees attracted the attention of the European and larger world media, as well as financial support from various NGOs and, in particular, from the United Nations, which channelled over $15

Illegal dwellings built by Crimean Tatars on the outskirts of Simferopol, 2012.

142

million through its Crimea Integration and Development Program, set up in 1994 specifically to alleviate some of the worst conditions in Tatar settlements.[5]

The stabilization in the relationship between independent Ukraine and its Autonomous Republic of Crimea following the adoption of constitutions by each entity did not enhance the political status of the Crimean Tatars. Neither the Kurultay nor Mejlis was given constitutional recognition, nor were Crimean Tatars recognized as the peninsula's indigenous people. Questions of property restitution and land rights were not addressed in either constitution, and while the Crimean Tatar language could be used in schools, no provisions were made for state funding. For a short period (1994-1998), the Tatars were guaranteed 14 seats in the Crimean parliament, but they lost this advantage following the adoption of a majority electoral system based on single mandates (1998) and then a proportional system (2006). Finally, as late as 1999, nearly half of Crimea's Tatars still lacked normal housing and 33 percent of able-bodied males were unemployed—the highest among all peoples in the peninsula.[6]

Such difficult conditions have produced periodic protests that have taken the form of clashes with local police, blockades of roads, and storming the building of the Crimean parliament in Simferopol.[7] The commemorations of the 1944 deportation, held annually on the "Black Day" (18 May) at various places throughout Crimea, continue to draw thousands of Tatars who protest peacefully with demands for the fulfillment of their long-standing grievances. Some newly founded organizations, such as the Union of Crimean Tatar Officers and Union of Crimean Turks, have suggested the need for more violent means to attain their demands. Such reactions reflect, in part, deeper problems within Crimean Tatar society: growing differences among various political factions; and the alienation and rejection by the younger generation of traditional community norms, including unquestioning acceptance of one's elders.

Nevertheless, it is the Kurultay and its executive body, the Mejlis, which remain the main political institutions representing Crimean Tatar interests. And these bodies, under the leadership of Mustafa Dzhemilev and Refat Chubarov, continue to maintain a moderate approach based on the belief that the best allies for the Crimean Tatar cause are those elements in Ukraine's political spectrum that are national-democratic in their political orientation. It is, therefore, not surprising that the Crimean Tatars elected to the national parliament in Kyiv (including Dzhemilev) have been candidates of the RUKH and Our Ukraine coalitions as well as other political forces in support of Ukraine's independence and European integration.

Perhaps more important than political activity is the need for cultural reclamation. This has taken various forms. While they were in Central Asia, it was the family which kept a sense of Crimean Tatarness alive. Mothers and grandmothers, in particular, taught the new

Simferopol. Seat of the Mejlis, the executive body of the Crimean Tatar Kurultay.

generations born in exile how to prepare dishes representative of Tatar national cuisine and to remember their ancestral homeland through traditional songs in the Crimean Tatar language. Like post-Holocaust Jews, who since World War II have been repeatedly reminded of the annihilation of their ancestors, so too were the young Tatars born in exile constantly reminded of the Sürgün, their people's deportation and exile in Soviet Central Asia.

Among the most important identity markers for Crimean Tatars are religion and language. The reality is that after half a century of deportation and an even longer period of Soviet repression of religion, Crimea's Tatars have, in general, only a passive relationship to both their religion and language. Some of the basic tenets of Islam (the prohi-

bition against alcohol and daily prayer obligations) are ignored, while most Tatars communicate among themselves as well as with others, not in the language of their ancestors, but in Russian. Language assimilation is, in part, the result of another widespread phenomenon: the high number of intermarriages between Crimean Tatars and persons outside the community. On the other hand, the predominance of such secular attitudes has provoked a number of young people to adopt a traditionalist (critics say fundamentalist) Muslim way in life. But such people are in the decided minority.

There have been efforts to rectify the severe shortage of mosques, Muslim clerics, schools, and institutions which promote the Crimean Tatar language and cultural heritage. Nevertheless, while the reasons may differ, the

144

fact remains that neither the autonomous republic nor the central Ukrainian authorities in Kyiv have done much to support Crimean Tatar (or for that matter Crimean Ukrainian) cultural endeavours. One outstanding exception is the extensive funding allocated by Ukraine's Ministry of Culture to restore the eighteenth-century Crimean khan's palace in Bakhchysaray. On the other hand, there are only 13 state elementary schools serving 4,000 students in which the language of instruction is Crimean Tatar.[8]

In the absence of any meaningful Ukrainian state funding, Crimean Tatar cultural activists have managed to attract private and public sector international support from several countries, including funds from the Netherlands for the Gaspirali Crimean Tatar National Library in Simferopol. The most important source of assistance, however, has been Turkey where, in part as a result of lobbying by the country's large Crimean Tatar diaspora, the government-funded Turkish Cooperation and Coordination Agency and the non-governmental Kirim (Crimea) Foundation has provided several million dollars in aid. The funds have been used for the purchase of medical supplies and building houses for individual families, as well as for the construction or reconstruction of several mosques, historical monuments such as the famed sixteenth-century Zinjirli *medrese* (Islamic theological academy) near Bakhchysaray, and schools such as the large elementary/secondary complex in Staryi Krym. Among the newest institutions is the La Richesse Crimean Historical Museum housed in the nineteenth-century *medrese* building in Starosillya/Salachik, just east of Bakhchysaray.

Cultural reclamation has not been limited to Crimea's Tatars. For example, the Karaites have restored the monuments connected with their two major centers: the mountain-top city of Chufut Kale and the Karaite district of Yevpatoriya. But most extensive of all cultural reclamation projects are those connected with the Ukrainian Orthodox Church of the Moscow Patriarchate. Beginning in the 1990s, a whole series of Orthodox churches and monasteries which for more than seventy years had been closed and neglected under Soviet rule were carefully and lovingly restored, not simply as architectural monuments from the past, but as living centers of Eastern Christian worship for monks and the faithful at large. Among the most ambitious of the reconstruction projects are those at the cave monasteries built into cliffs: the Dormition Monastery near Bakhchysaray and the Inkerman Monastery just opposite Sevastopol. The culmination of the efforts to restore Crimea to its nineteenth-century status as the "Mount Athos of the Russian world" was the reconstruction of the St. Vladimir Cathedral on the alleged spot in ancient Chersonesus/Kherson where Grand Prince Vladimir was baptized as the first step in the late-ninth-century Christianization of Rus'. This monumental project completed in 2002 was made possible with extensive funds provided by the governments of both Ukraine and Russia.

The laudable campaigns of historic and cultural reclamation carried on with great intensity in Crimea since the period of Ukraine's independence in 1991 have not been without controversy. For example, a new market place may be planned on a spot that is sacred to the Crimean Tatars, or the expansion of an Orthodox monastery complex may be infringing on a Karaite cemetery. Such controversies are inevitable, given the fact that the Crimean landscape is laden—some might say overburdened—with secular and religious monuments built by the region's various inhabitants going back nearly three-thousand years.

Such cultural battles inevitably lead to the question: to whom does this land belong? The answer should be obvious. Crimea is the common patrimony of all peoples past and present who have ever lived on its territory. Therefore, today's inhabitants have a duty to respect and promote the cultures, religions, languages, and civic aspirations of all peoples, regardless of their numerical size, who still call Crimea their home. Autonomous status within Ukraine, together with ongoing efforts to promote mutual respect among the peninsula's inhabitants, would seem to be the best means for Crimea to become, indeed, a blessed land.

In February 2014, the Russian Federation headed by President Vladimir Putin forcibly annexed Crimea. Russia's act, condemned by the international community, was part of a larger policy aimed at destabilizing Ukraine in the hope of bringing it back within Russia's larger geopolitical sphere that covers much of Eurasia.

Since 2014, tens of thousands of Crimea's ethnic Ukrainians have fled north and now live as refugees in various parts of Ukraine. The region's Crimean Tatars, who were exiled en masse in 1944 and who struggled so hard to return home in the 1990s, were not about to leave their homeland once again. While most have stayed in Crimea and are trying to accommodate as best they can to the Russian regime, their political and civic leaders have suffered for their beliefs. The Crimean Tatar national assembly (Kurultay) and its executive organ (Mejlis) were forcibly closed, its leading figures including Mustafa Dzhemilev and Refat Chubarov were barred from returning to Crimea, and many of the Crimean Tatar civic and media activists who opposed Russian rule have been arrested. In several cases, they have simply disappeared. Crimean Tatar language schools, newspapers, and other media outlets have been shut down by the new Russian authorities.

As history teaches us all, states come and go, but peoples remain. The Crimean Tatars have chosen to remain in their ancestral homeland, Crimea, which inevitably will one day be returned to where it belongs—Ukraine.

The Crimean Tatars are here to stay

The disastrous deportation and exile of Crimea's Tatars in 1944 and their return home nearly half a century later is an epic story that has impressed and inspired observers the world over. Among these is Neal Ascherson, a distinguished British journalist and specialist in central and eastern Europe who wrote the following in the early 1990s, when tensions were still running high:

At last, the Tatars are returning home. They call it home, although fifty years constitutes more than a human generation and all but a minority of those who return were born in Kazakhstan and Uzbekistan. They call it home, but the small white-plastered cottages smothered in vine arbours which belonged to them or to their parents or grandparents are now occupied by Russian or Ukrainian immigrants who, for the most part, hate them. They are attacked by their neighbours, and there have been murders. They are treated as alien squatters by the corrupt Crimean regional government which currently rules at Simferopol. But on stony valley-bottoms which nobody wants, on the barren waste lots outside the Crimean cities, men and women are building houses out of home-made clay bricks, reeds, and corrugated iron. They measure up and parcel out the barren land between families, and conjure water out of the rocks. There is a haze of green seedlings where once was only dusty grey turf, and a din of hammering. This is their Israel, their promised land, and they will not be parted from it again.

SOURCE: Neal Ascherson, Black Sea (New York, 1995), p. 33.

Crimean Tatar young girl in national dress.

NOTES

Chapter 1: **What is Crimea?**

1. Neal Ascherson, *Black Sea* (New York, 1995), p.24.

Chapter 4: **The Crimean Khanate**

1. Cited in Mykhailo Hrushevsky, *History of Ukraine-Rus'*, Vol. VIII: *The Cossack Age, 1626-1650* (Edmonton and Toronto, 2002), p. 535.

2. Alan Fisher, *The Crimean Tatars* (Stanford, Calif., 1978), p. 25.

3. There is much controversy on the numbers of captives taken. See the discussion of the literature on this question in Thomas M. Prymak, "Tatar Slave Raiding and Turkish Captivity in Ukrainian History and Legend" (unpublished manuscript).

Chapter 5: **Crimea in the Russian Empire**

1. Alan Fisher, *The Crimean Tatars* (Stanford, Calif., 1978), p. 78.

2. Cited in George Vernadsky et. al., eds., *A Source Book for Russian History from Early Times to 1917*, Vol. II (New Haven, Conn., 1972), p. 72.

3. Fisher, *Crimean Tatars*, p. 93.

4. Andrii Kozyts'kyi, *Henotsyd ta polityka masovoho vynyshchennia tsyvil'noho naselennia u XX st.* (L'viv, 2012), p. 363; Hakan Kirimli, *National Movements and National Identity Among the Crimean Tatars, 1905-1916* (Leiden, New York, and Köln, 1996), pp. 10-11.

5. Brian Glynn Williams, *The Crimean Tatars: The Diaspora Experience and the Forging of a Nation* (Leiden, Boston, and Köln, 2001), p. 244.

6. Tetiana B. Bykova, *Stvorennia Kryms'koï ASRR, 1917-1921 rr.* (Kyiv, 2011), p. 33.

7. Innokentiy's proposal was formally called, "Notes about the Restoration of Ancient Holy Places in the Crimean Mountains," and is discussed in Mara Kozelsky, *Christianizing in the Russian Empire and Beyond* (De Kalb, Ill., 2010), pp. 62-88.

Chapter 6: **Crimea in War and Revolution**

1. Tetiana B. Bykova, *Stvorennia Kryms'koï ASRR, 1917-1921 rr.* (Kyiv, 2011), p. 119.

Chapter 7:
The Crimean Autonomous Soviet Socialist Republic

1. Cited in Valerii P. Diulichev, *Krym: istoriia v ocherkakh—XX vek* (Simferopol, 2006), p. 101.

2. Ibid., p. 117

3. Stanislav Kul'chyts'kyi, "Kryms'ke pytannia v konteksti politychnoï istoriï XX storichchia," in *Natsional'ne pytannia v Ukraïni XX—pochatku XXI st.: istorychni narysy* (Kyiv, 2012), p. 522.

4. Paul Robert Magocsi, *A History of Ukraine: The Land and Its Peoples,* 2nd revised and expanded ed. (Toronto, 2010), p. 621.

5. Diulichev, *Krym—XX vek,* p. 145.

6. Ibid.

7. Ibid., pp. 146-147.

8. Ibid., p. 127.

9. Alan Fisher, *The Crimean Tatars* (Stanford, Calif., 1978), p. 142.

10. Ibid., p. 141.

11. Report of T. Lordkiparidze, head of the NKVD in Crimea, to the 18th Conference of the Communist party of the Crimean A.S.S.R., cited in Diulichev, *Krym—XX vek,* pp. 141-142.

Chapter 8: **Crimea during World War II**

1. Alan Fisher, *The Crimean Tatars* (Stanford, Calif., 1978), p. 152.

2. The figures provided in the paragraph are drawn from sometimes differing data in J. Otto Pohl, *Ethnic Cleansing in the USSR, 1937-1949* (Westport, Conn., 1999), p. 112; Server Tairov, *Krymskie tatary v drevneishikh vremen do nashikh dnei* (Simferopol', 2011), p. 415-416; and Andrii Kozyts'kyi, *Henotsyd ta polityka masovoho vynyshchennia tsyvil'noho naselennia u XX st.* (Lviv, 2012), p. 364-365.

3. Ibid., p. 366; Fisher, *Crimean Tatars,* p. 156; and Jonathan Dekel-Chen, "Crimea," in Gershon David Hundert, ed., *The YIVO Encyclopedia of Jews in Eastern Europe,* Vol. I (New Haven and London, 2008), p. 364.

4. Letter of A. Mokrousov and the secretary of the Simferopol Committee of the Communist party, S. Martinov, dated July 1942, cited in Kozyts'kyi, *Henotsyd,* p. 366.

5. Of the 3,783 Soviet partisans in Crimea in early 1944, there were 630 Crimean Tatars, or 16.6 percent of the total. According to the most recent previous census (1938) in Crimea, the Tatars comprised 19.3 percent of the peninsula's population. Pohl, *Ethnic Cleansing in the USSR,* pp. 112-113.

6. Soviet State Defense Committee Resolution No. 5959ss, dated 11 May 1944 and signed by J. Stalin, cited in ibid., p.112.

7. Several thousand more Crimean Tatars were found during the next few weeks, so that by June 9 the number deported rose to 188,600. Valerii Diulichev, *Krym: istoriia v ocherkakh—XX vek* (Simferopol, 2006), p. 236.

8. Cited in Ènver Ozenbashly, *Krymtsy,* 2nd rev. ed. (Akmesdzhit/Simferopol, 2006), p. 21.

9. Kozyts'kyi, *Henotsyd,* p. 371-372. It is interesting to note that during the brief presence of the Soviet Army in eastern Crimea in 1942, the last of Crimea's 438 Italians were deported to Soviet Kazakhstan.

10. Diulchev, *Krym—XX vek,* p. 237.

Chapter 9: **Soviet Crimea and Exiled Crimean Tatars**

1. The figures provided by one author include the destruction of 360 village reading rooms, 263 clubs, 900 schools, and 1,263 libraries—including those in private hands (112), in elementary and secondary schools (861), in village cooperatives (200), as well as regional and city libraries (90). Andrii Kozyts'kyi, *Henotsyd ta polityka masovoho vynyshchennia tsyvil'noho naselennia u XX st.* (Lviv, 2012), p. 370-371.

2. "Krymskaia oblast'," in *Bolshaia sovetskaia èntsyklopediia,* 2nd ed., Vol. XXIII (Moscow, 1953), p. 552.

3. P. N. Nadinskii, *Ocherki po istorii Kryma,* Vol. I (Simferopol, 1951)—the passage from this now rare Soviet Marxist volume is cited in Ludmilla Alexeyeva, "Mustafa Jemiloglu [Dzhemelev], His Character and Convictions," in Edward A. Allworth, ed., *The Tatars of Crimea: Return to the Homeland:*

Studies and Documents, 2nd rev. ed. (Durham, N. C. and London, 1998), p. 208.

4. As reported by S. Seliuk, "Za glubokoe izuchenie istorii rodiny," *Pravda* (Moscow), 4 June 1952, p.2.

5. The idea of Crimea as a gift may be nothing more than Soviet mythology. See the discussion in Gwendolyn Sasse, *The Crimea Question: Identity, Transition, and Conflict* (Cambridge, Mass., 2007), pp. 107-121.

6. Valerii P. Diulichev, *Krym: istoriia v ocherkakh—XX vek* (Simferopol', 2006), p. 196.

7. Serhii Chornyi, *Natsional'nyi sklad naselennia Ukraïny v XX storichchi: dovidnyk* (Kyiv, 2001), p. 76.

8. Kozyts'kyi, *Henotsyd,* p. 370.

9. The statistical data in the following paragraphs on industrial and agricultural developments are taken from Diulichev, *Krym—XX vek,* pp. 254-262.

10. The statistics on resorts and tourism are from the entry "Crimea," in *Encyclopedia of Ukraine,* Vol. I, ed. Volodymyr Kubijovyč (Toronto, 1984), p. 617.

11. J. Otto Pohl, *Ethnic Cleansing in the USSR, 1937-1949* (Westport, Conn., 1999), p. 115. Statistics from 1953 identify 165,000 Crimean Tatars in Soviet Central Asia, 78 percent of whom resided in Soviet Uzbekistan. See the table in ibid., p. 116.

12. Cited in Alan Fisher, *The Crimean Tatars* (Stanford, Calif., 1978), p. 176.

13. Decree of the Presidium of the Supreme Soviet of the USSR, cited in ibid., p. 179.

14. From Hryhorenko's pamphlet, "Who are the Criminals?," sent in March 1969 to the Politburo in Moscow, cited in ibid., p. 197.

15. Brian Glynn Williams, *The Crimean Tatars: The Diaspora Experience and the Forging of a Nation* (Leiden, Boston, and Köln, 2001), p. 448.

16. Sasse, *The Crimea Question,* pp.137-138.

Chapter 10: **Crimea in Independent Ukraine**

1. "Konstitutsiia Avtonomnoi Respubliki Krym," cited in Valerii P. Diulichev, *Krym: istoriia v ocherkakh—XX vek* (Simferopol, 2006), p. 295.

2. Gwendolyn Sasse, *The Crimea Question: Identity, Transition, and Conflict* (Cambridge, Mass., 2007), p. 225.

3. Vladimir Kazarin, cited in Open Society Institute, *Crimean Tatars: Repatriation and Conflict Prevention* (New York, N.Y., 1996), p. 71.

4. Brian Glynn Williams, *The Crimean Tatars: The Diaspora Experience and the Forging of a Nation* (Leiden, Boston, and Köln, 2001), p. 448-454; International Court of Justice, The Hague, *Counter-Memorial ... Submitted by the Russian Federation* (9 August 2021), Annex 21: Expert Report, p. 82.

5. Open Society Institute, *Crimean Tatars*, p. 79.

6. Sasse, *The Crimea Question,* p. 190.

7. The attacks on Crimea's parliament, which took place between 1 and 6 October 1992, were prompted by the arrest of several Crimean Tatars in an arbitrary manner in the village of Krasnyi Rai, near Alushta.

8. Another 35,500 students have access to some subjects taught in Crimean Tatar in schools in which the language of instruction is Russian. These figures, from the 2002-2003 school year, are found in Volodymyr B. Ievtukh et al., *Etnonatsional'na struktura ukraïnskoho suspil'stva* (Kyiv, 2004), p. 16.

FOR FURTHER READING
(A select English-language bibliography)

Allworth, Edward A., ed., *The Tatars of Crimea: Return to the Homeland.* 2nd revised and expanded ed. Durham, N.C. and London: Duke University Press, 1998.

Ascherson, Neal. *Black Sea.* New York: Hill and Wang, 1996.

Brett, C. E. B. *Towers of Crim Tatary: English and Scottish Architects and Craftsmen in the Crimea, 1762-1853.* Donnington, U. K.: Shaun Tyas, 2005.

Chase, Philip. "Conflict in Crimea: An Examination of Ethnic Conflict under the Contemporary Model of Sovereignty," *Columbia Journal of Transnational Law,* XXXIV, 1 (New York, 1996), pp. 219-254.

Curtis, John Shelton. *Russia's Crimean War.* Durham. N. C.: Duke University Press, 1979.

Czapliński, Władysław et al., eds. *The Case of Crimea's Annexation under International Law.* Warsaw: Scholar Publishing House, 2017.

Dekel-Chen, Jonathan L. *Farming the Red Land: Jewish Agricultural Colonization and Local Soviet Power, 1924-1941.* New Haven and London: Yale University Press, 2005.

Figes, Orlando. *The Crimean War: A History.* New York, N.Y.: Metropolitan Books/Henry Holt, 2010.

Fisher, Alan W. *The Crimean Tatars.* Stanford, Calif.: Hoover Institute Press, 1978.

_____. "Emigration of Muslims from the Russia Empire in the Years after the Crimean War," *Jarbücher für Geschichte Osteuropas,* XXXV, 3 (Wiesbaden, 1987), pp. 356-371.

_____. "Muscovy and the Black Sea Slave Trade," *Canadian-American Slavic Studies,* VI, 4 (Pittsburgh, 1972), pp. 575-594.

_____. *The Russian Annexation of the Crimea, 1772-1783.* Cambridge: Cambridge University Press, 1970.

_____. "Shahin Giray, the Reformer Khan, and the Russian Annexation of the Crimea," *Jarbücher für Geschichte Osteuropas,* N. S., XV, 4 (Wiesbaden, 1967), pp. 375-394.

Guboglo, M. N. and Chervonnaia, S. M. "The Crimean Tatar Question and the Present Ethnopolitical Situation in Crimea," *Russian Politics and Law* (Armonk, N.Y., 1995), pp. 31-60.

Jemilev, Mustafa. *Crimean Tatars: Problems and Prospects.* Simferopol': Odzhak, 2010.

Khazanov, Anatoly. *The Krymchaks: A Vanishing Group in the Soviet Union.* Research Paper No. 71. Jerusalem: Hebrew University of Jerusalem, 1989.

Kirimli, Edige. "The Crimean Tatars," *Studies on the Soviet Union,* N. S., X, 1 (Munich, 1970), pp. 70-97.

Kirimli, Hakan. *National Movements and National Identity among the Crimean Tatars, 1905-1916.* Leiden, New York, and Köln: E. J. Brill, 1996.

Kozelsky, Mara. "Casualties of Conflict: Crimean Tatars during the Crimean War," *Slavic Review,* LXVII, 4 (Cambridge, Mass., 2008), pp. 866-891.

_____. *Christianizing Crimea: Shaping Sacred Space in the Russian Empire and Beyond.* De Kalb, Ill.: Northern Illinois University Press, 2010.

Kuzio, Taras. *Ukraine—Crimea—Russia: Triangle of Conflict.* Stuttgart: Ibidem Vlg., 2007.

Lazzerini, Edward. "Crimean Tatar: the Fate of a Severed Tongue." In Isabelle T. Kreindler, ed. *Sociolinguistic Perspectives on Soviet National Languages.* Berlin, New York, and Amsterdam: Mouton de Gruyter, 1985, pp. 109-124.

_____. "Ismail Bey Gasprinskii's *Perevodchik/Turcüman:* A Clarion Call of Modernism." In Hasan Paksoy, ed. *Central Asian Monuments.* Istanbul: Isis Press, 1992, pp. 143-156.

Lazzerini, Edward J. "Local Accommodation and Resistance to Colonialism in Nineteenth-Century

Crimea." In Daniel R. Brower and Edward J. Lazzerini, eds., *Russia's Orient: Imperial Border-lands and Peoples, 1700-1917.* Bloomington, Ind.: Indiana University Press, 1997, pp. 169-187.

Mack, Glenn R. and Joseph Coleman Carter, eds. *Crimean Chersonesos: City, Chora, Museum, and Environs.* Austin, Tex.: University of Texas, Institute of Classical Archaeology, 2003.

Marples, David R. and David F. Duke. "Ukraine, Russia, and the Question of Crimea," *Nationalities Papers,* XXIII, 2 (Abington, Eng., 1995), pp. 261-289.

Mungo, Melvin. "The Campaign in Crimea." In Melvin Mungo. *Manstein: Hitler's Greatest General.* London: Weidenfeld and Nicolson, 2010, pp. 227-273.

O'Neill, Kelly Ann. *Claiming Crimea: A History of Catherine the Great's Southern Empire.* New Haven and London: Yale University Press, 2017.

_____. "Constructing Imperial Identity in the Borderland: Architecture, Islam, and the Reno-vation of the Crimean Landscape," *Ad Imperio,* VII, 2 (Kazan, 2006), pp. 163-191.

Ozhiganov, Edward. "The Crimean Republic: Rivalries for Control." In Alexei Arbatov et al., eds. *Managing Conflict in the Former Soviet Union.* Cambridge, Mass.: MIT Press, 1997, pp. 83-136.

Plokhy, Serhii. "The City of Glory: Sevastopol in Russian Historical Mythology," *Journal of Contem-porary History,* XXXV, 3 (London, 2000), pp. 369-384.

Polliack, Meira, ed. *Karaite Judaism: A Guide to Its History and Literary Sources.* Leiden and Boston: Brill, 2003, esp. the chapters in the section "Eastern Europe and the Crimea," pp. 633-818.

Rostovtzeff, Michael. *Iranians and Greeks in South Russia.* Oxford: Oxford University Press, 1922.

Sasse, Gwendolyn. "The Crimean Issue," *Journal of Communist Studies and Transitional Politics,* XII, 1 (London, 1996), pp. 83-116.

_____. *The Crimean Question: Identity, Transition, and Conflict.* Cambridge, Mass.: Harvard University Press/Harvard Ukrainian Research Institute, 2007.

Schütz, Edmond. "The *Tat* People in the Crimea," *Acta Orientalia Academiae,* XXXI, 1 (Budapest, 1977), pp. 77-106.

Seytmurova, Ayshe. *Mustafa Dzhemilev and the Crimea Tatars: The Story of the Man and His People.* New York: Center for Democracy, 1986.

Torbakov, Igor B. "Russian-Ukrainian Relations 1917-1918: A Conflict over Crimea and the Black Sea Fleet," *Nationalities Papers,* XXIV, 4 (Abington, Eng., 1996), pp. 679-689.

Tuna, Mustafa Özgür. "Gaspirali v. Il'minskii: Two Identity Projects for the Muslims of the Russian Empire," *Nationalities Papers,* XXX, 2 (Basingstoke, Eng., 2002), pp. 265-289.

Ueling, Greta Lynn. *Beyond Memory: The Crimean Tatars' Deportation and Return.* New York: Pal-grave Macmillan, 2004.

_____. "The Crimean Tatars in Uzbekistan: Speaking with the Dead and Living Homeland, *Central Asian Survey,* XX, 3 (Basingstoke, Eng., 2001), pp. 391-404.

_____. "Squatting, Self-Immolation, and the Repatriation of Crimean Tatars," *Nationalities Papers,* XXVIII, 2 (Basingstoke, Eng., 2000), pp. 317-341.

Vasiliev, Alexander A. *The Goths in the Crimea.* Cambridge, Mass.: Medieval Academy of America, 1936.

Williams, Brian Glyn. "A Community Re-imagined: The Role of 'Homeland' in the Forging of a Na-tional Identity: The Case of the Crimean Tatars," *Journal of Muslim Minority Affairs,* XVII, 2 (Abington, Eng., 1997), pp. 225-252.

_____. *The Crimean Tatars: The Diaspora Experience and the Forging of a Nation.* Leiden, New York, and Köln: E. J. Brill, 2001.

_____. "The Ethnogenesis of the Crimean Tatars: An Historical Reinterpretation," *Journal of the Royal Asiatic Society:* Series 3, XI, 3 (London, 2001), pp. 329-348.

ILLUSTRATION SOURCES AND CREDITS

Contemporary photographs created especially for this publication by:
© **Valerii Padiak**
(pages 5, 7, 10, 16, 17, 20, 21, 23, 24, 28, 30, 32, 34, 38, 42, 45, 54, 61, 70, 98, 135, 136, 142, 144, 147)

Other photographs, in the context of the Wiki Loves Earth competition are by
© **Serhii Krynytsya** (pages 1 and 6) and © **Ihor Derevyahin** (page 2).

Other documentary and journalistic photographs are by B. Bochkovskyi (page 67), V. Yeremenko (page 71), Vlastar (page 128), the Crimean Tatar newspaper *Avdet* (page 145), the Crimean Tatar journal *Bahçesaray* (page 122), the publication *Radost i bol vozvrashcheniya / Bittersweet of Homecoming* (Simferopol, 2010, pages 134 and 140), and other archival photographs without attribution.

The publisher expresses its appreciation to the Crimean Tatar Mejlis in Simferopol and, in particular, to its former chairman Mustafa Dzhemilev for assistance in the publication of this volume, as well as to the following institutions for permission to use illustrative material from their collections:

Bakhchysaray Historical and Cultural Reserve

    • Salachyk Museum

    • Gaspirali/Gasprinskii Memorial Center

Kerch State Historical and Cultural Reserve

Gasprinskii Crimean Tatar Library in Simferopol

La Richesse Crimean Tatar Historical Museum in Bakhchysaray

Aivazovskii National Art Gallery in Feodosiya

Taurian Central Museum in Simferopol

Taurian Chersonesus Cultural Reserve in Sevastopol

The author is very grateful to the following individuals who read critically the unpublished version of this book and offered their scholarly and editorial comments:

Feliz Tutku Aydin (University of Toronto), **John Jaworsky** (University of Waterloo), **Nadiya Kushko** (University of Toronto), **Taras Kuzio** (School of Advanced International Studies, John Hopkins University), **Lubomyr Luciuk** (Royal Military College of Canada), **Victor Ostapchuk** (University of Toronto), **Thomas M. Prymak** (University of Toronto), and **Richard Ratzlaff** (University of Toronto Press).